Bass

For the Bassist looking to progress their skills and knowledge

By Gareth Evans

ISBN 978-0-9576506-1-9

Written by Gareth Evans

Photography, Diagrams and Cover design by Gareth Evans

Additional Illustrations by Chris Evans

Copyright © 2013 by Intuition Publications

www.guitar-book.com

International Copyright Secured. All rights reserved. No part of this publication may be reproduced in any form or by any means without the prior written permission of the publisher

Audio Tracks

These can be downloaded for free from   www.intuition-books.com

1	E Major Blues	(Demo)
2	E Major Blues	(Backing)
3	Roots	(Demo)
4	Roots	(Backing)
5	Roots and Octaves	(Demo)
6	Roots and Octaves	(Backing)
7	Roots and 5ths	(Demo)
8	Roots and 5ths	(Backing)
9	Power Chords	(Demo)
10	Power Chords	(Backing)
11	Bossa Bassa	(Demo)
12	Bossa Bassa	(Backing)
13	Major Arpeggios	(Demo)
14	Major Arpeggios	(Backing)
15	Minor Arpeggios	(Demo)
16	Minor Arpeggios	(Backing)
17	Major and Minor	(Demo)
18	Major and Minor	(Backing)
19	Rock Riff 1	(Demo)
20	Rock Riff 1	(Backing)
21	Rock Riff 2	(Demo)
22	Rock Riff 2	(Backing)
23	Bayou Noir	(Demo)
24	Bayou Noir	(Backing)
25	Calm Beach	(Demo)
26	Calm Beach	(Backing)
27	Rock Riff 3	(Demo)
28	Rock Riff 3	(Backing)
29	Major 7th Arpeggios	(Demo)
30	Major 7th Arpeggios	(Backing)
31	Minor 7th Arpeggios	(Demo)
32	Minor 7th Arpeggios	(Backing)
33	Dominant 7th…	(Demo)
34	Dominant 7th…	(Backing)
35	7th Arpeggios	(Demo)
36	7th Arpeggios	(Backing)
37	7th Arpeggios (2)	(Demo)
38	7th Arpeggios (2)	(Backing)
39	Heist	(Demo)
40	Heist	(Backing)
41	Mo' Slap n Pop	(Demo)
42	Mo' Slap n Pop	(Backing)
43	70's Mystery	(Demo)
44	70's Mystery	(Backing)
45	Flow	(Demo)
46	Flow	(Backing)
47	Slides	(Demo)
48	Slides	(Backing)
49	Slidey	(Demo)
50	Slidey	(Backing)
51	Slapato	(Demo)
52	Slapato	(Backing)
53	Encounters…	(Demo)
54	A Day to Remember	(Demo)
55	A Day to Remember	(Backing)
56	Over the Hills…	(Demo)
57	Over the Hills…	(Backing)
58	Tapestry	(Demo)
59	Storm before the Calm	(Demo)
60	Storm before the Calm	(Backing)

Introduction

This book is for beginners and intermediate players looking to expand skills and knowledge in areas specific to the Bass. Depending on your experience some of the subjects, particularly earlier on, may already be familiar although there may be something you have missed and whatever your strengths are there might be other areas to be brought up to speed. The first half of chapter 1 is a primer some may need it, but feel free to skim ahead to page 12 if you wish.

Photographs, diagrams and illustrations are used to explain various aspects such as technique, theory and fret-board knowledge. Theory is explained using the actual fret-board to make it applicable and easier to relate to. Musical pieces of various styles are used to make the learning process more practical and enjoyable. The pieces are a guide but can be adapted by more experienced players by making their own Bass-lines using the given structure.

Each audio track has two versions, a demo track to show how the piece should sound, followed by a backing track for you to play over where the Bass guitar has been removed.

The rhythmical aspect of sight-reading is covered, as tablature doesn't indicate this. Toward the back of the book the theory becomes more advanced and there is an introduction to further techniques such as Slap n' Pop and Tapping.

The final Chapter has stretching exercises and tips on how to practise. You don't need to wait until you have finished the book to read that section, as the advice can be useful from the beginning.

Contents

Chapter 1 - The Beginning

The Bass Guitar…………………	6
Tuning the Bass…………………	7 - 8
Basic Technique…………………	8 - 9
Tablature………………………	9 - 10
Fret-board Diagrams……………	11
Introduction to Sight-reading……	12
Plucking Techniques……………	13 - 17
Fretting Hand Technique…………	18 - 19
E Major Blues…………………	20
Questions………………………	21

Chapter 2 - Fundamentals

Fret-board Layout…………………	22 - 23
Creating Bass Lines………………	24 - 26
The Structure of Music……………	27 - 30
Fretting Exercise…………………	31 - 33
Fundamental Major Scale Shapes	34 - 36
Transposing by the Root Note……	37 - 38
Arpeggios…………………………	39 - 46
Developing Plucking Technique….	47 - 48
Questions…………………………	49

Chapter 3 - Reading Rhythm

Sight-reading……………………	50 - 53
How to Keep Time………………	54 - 55
Rhythm Exercises………………	56 - 58
Dotted Notes……………………	59
Tied Notes………………………	60
Sample Pieces…………………	61 - 65
Questions………………………	66

Chapter 4 - 7th Arpeggios

Major 7th .... 67 - 69
Minor 7th .... 69 - 71
Dominant 7th .... 71 - 72
7th Arpeggios............................ 73 - 74
Questions................................. 75

Chapter 5 - Modes and Harmony

Modes of the Major Scale .... 76 - 82
Modes of the Minor Scale............ 83
Harmonising............................. 84 - 88
Roman Numerals...................... 89 - 92
Questions................................. 93

Chapter 6 - Further Techniques

Slap and Pop........................... 94 - 97
Legato..................................... 98 - 101
Harmonics................................ 102 - 105
Tapping................................... 106 - 107
Questions................................. 108

Chapter 7 - Tips

How to Practise........................ 109 - 110
Stretching Exercises.................. 110 - 112
How to String a Bass................. 113 - 115
Answers................................... 116 - 118

1 The Beginning

The Bass Guitar

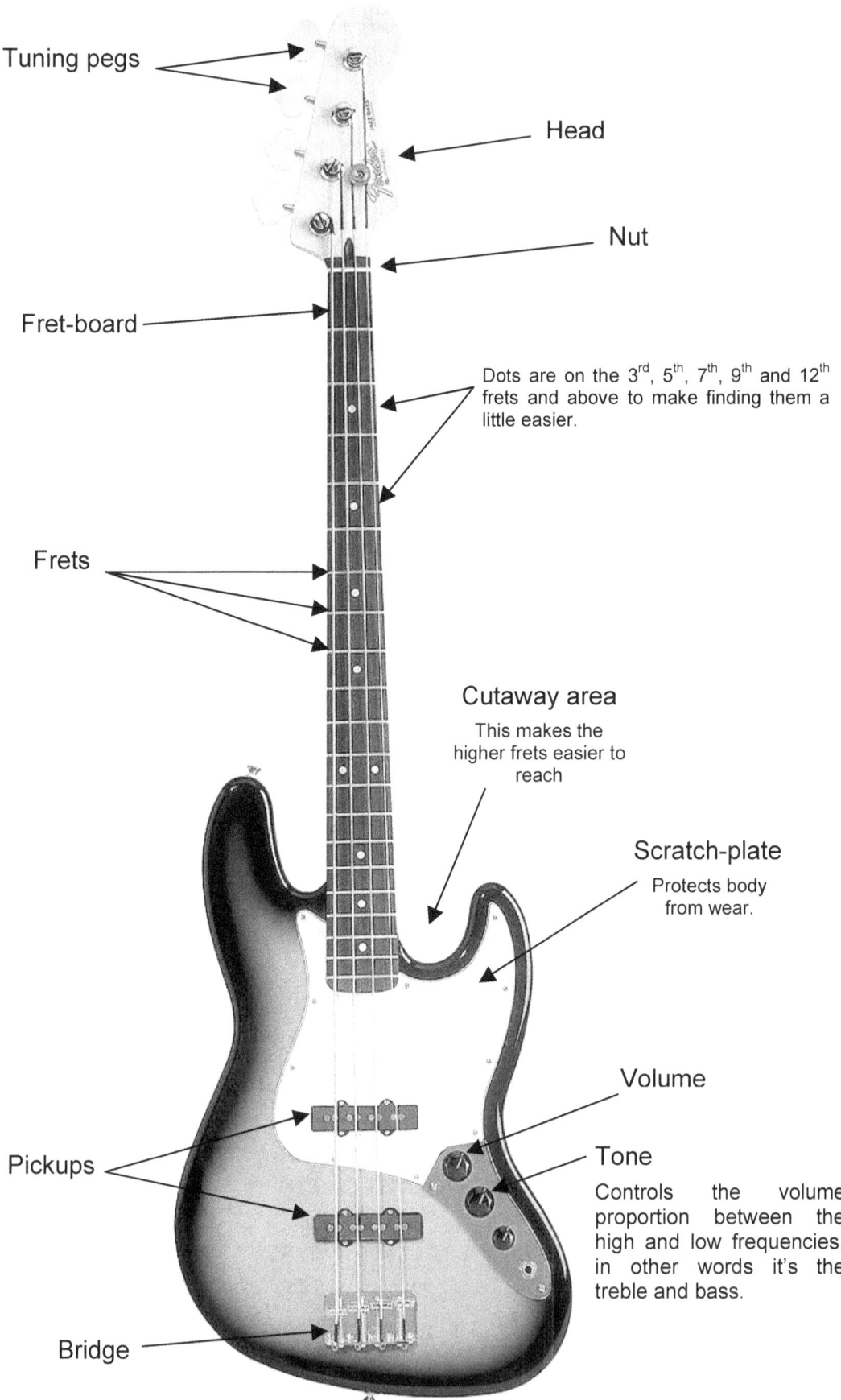

- Tuning pegs
- Head
- Nut
- Fret-board
- Dots are on the 3rd, 5th, 7th, 9th and 12th frets and above to make finding them a little easier.
- Frets
- Cutaway area
  This makes the higher frets easier to reach
- Scratch-plate
  Protects body from wear.
- Volume
- Tone
  Controls the volume proportion between the high and low frequencies, in other words it's the treble and bass.
- Pickups
- Bridge

Tuning the Bass

The strings are named according to what note they sound when played open. Open means a string is played on its own without the other hand pressing down on any of the frets.

Even though the low E string is positioned on top of the other strings it gives the lowest note, which is why it is called the "low E". The G is physically below the other strings and gives the highest note.

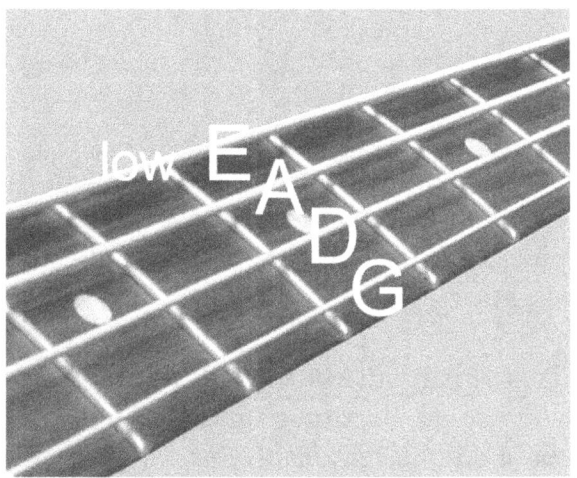

To make the string names easier to remember a mnemonic can be used such as "**E**very **A**ngry **D**og **G**rowls".

There are a number of ways to tune a Bass guitar. The easiest and most accurate is with an electronic tuner. An Electronic tuner can be plugged directly into the Bass. Most of these also have an internal microphone so they can be used to tune to the sound of an amplified Bass.

Another kind of electronic tuner is the clip-on tuner, which reads vibrations from the instrument. Distraction from other sounds will be minimal compared to using a microphone tuner.

Although using a tuner is accurate and good for situations like exams or performances. Another way is to tune the Bass by ear, which can develop your sound perception. For this you can tune to another instrument that is already in tune. Over the page is how you would refer to the keys of a piano or electronic keyboard…

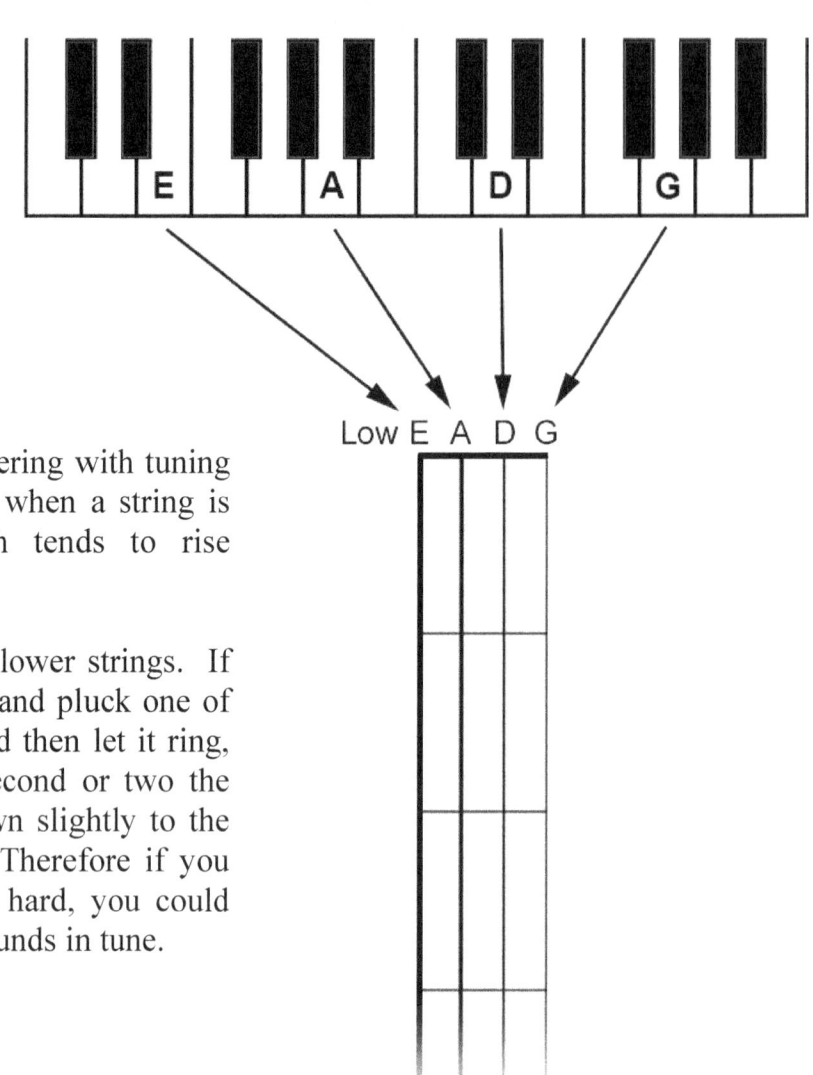

One last thing worth considering with tuning stringed instruments is that when a string is plucked, initially its pitch tends to rise slightly.

This is particularly true for lower strings. If you use an electronic tuner and pluck one of these strings reasonably hard then let it ring, you might notice after a second or two the dial of the tuner settles down slightly to the actual pitch of the string. Therefore if you are going to play the Bass hard, you could tune it slightly lower so it sounds in tune.

Basic Technique…How to hold the Bass

When sitting to play you should be upright with the Bass upright on your lap and its neck tilted upward slightly. Using a music stand at eye level for reading can also make it easier to maintain good posture and is more comfortable than crouching over your Bass to read music off a table or desk. Pegs can be used to hold pages open.

Sometimes when standing up to play, the Bass is slung low, usually for style. For the best position to play in however it is better not to have it slung too low otherwise it becomes difficult for your fretting hand to reach around the neck. Wearing a strap while sitting can also give extra stability and comfort.

To play any note the fretting finger should press the string down just behind the fret.

You needn't press *too* hard because whether you press quite hard or just hard enough the note will still be clear. You can find out by pressing a finger lightly on a fret while plucking the string, gradually increase the pressure until you hear a clear note, that's all the pressure you need. If you practise like this so it becomes how you play, then eventually you'll move around the fret-board easier without your fretting hand getting tired.

Try the same with all fingers from index to the little finger on different strings and frets.

Tablature

Tablature or "Tab" for short is a simple way of reading for the Bass guitar as it gives a graphical representation of the fret-board. The four horizontal lines represent the four strings of the Bass with the G string at the top and the low E string at the bottom. The following diagram lines a Bass guitar up next to some tablature to show this…

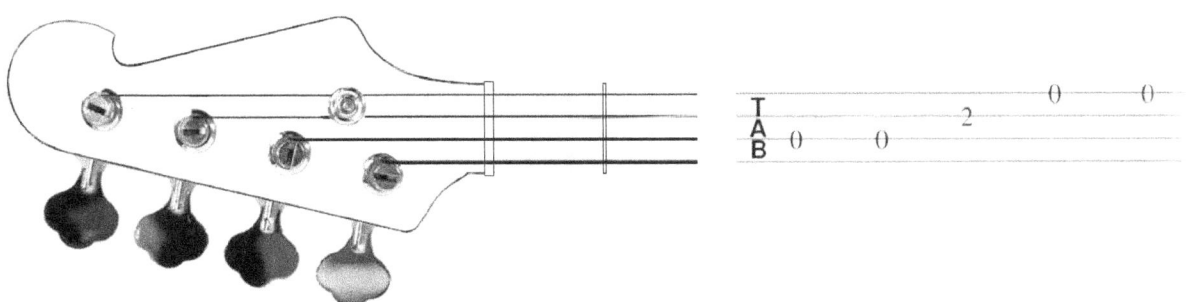

The numbers on the strings tell us what fret to play on, or if the string is to be played open when there is a "0". The above Tab is telling us to play the open A string twice then the 2nd fret of the D string, followed by the G string played open twice.

If you are wondering why it is "upside down" this is so that it matches conventional notation (explained later) which places higher pitched notes toward the top line and lower pitched notes toward the bottom line, hence for tablature the G string at the top and the low E string at the bottom to match. Another reason could be because when you look down at the Bass guitar on your lap while playing it, the highest string (G) is in the "top" of your field of vision because you are looking downward!

Here is a simple piece to play to get an idea of reading from tablature...

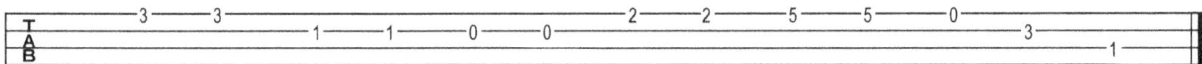

It is also important to consider what fingers we are using. The picture shows how the fingers of the fretting hand are numbered.

Below is the same melody with numbers added underneath to indicate what fingers should be used on the frets…

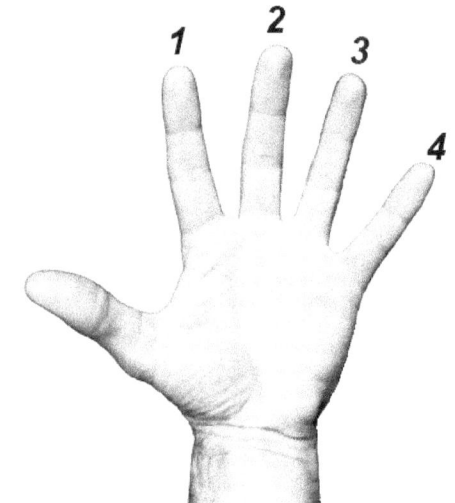

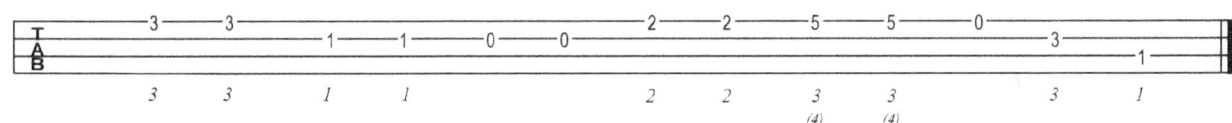

Within some parts of the book these numbers have been added where necessary to indicate what fingers should be used on which frets.

Fret-board Diagrams

These are used to show scales or arpeggios (covered later). Similar to tablature they give a graphical representation of the fret-board. In the diagram below, the horizontal lines represent the strings, which are shown the same way around as they are on the tablature. The thicker vertical line on the left is the nut and to the right of that are the frets from the 1st and upward.

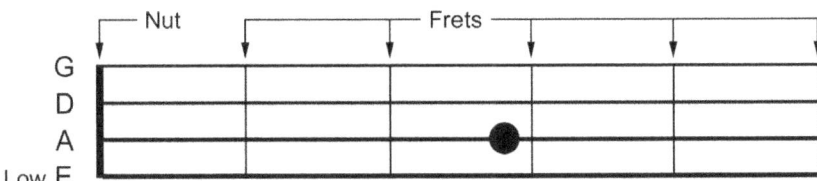

Dots are placed to show where the fretting fingers should be placed. In the diagram above, a dot has been placed on the third fret of the A string so you would place a finger there and play that note (which is C).

When further up the neck, a fret number is used to show where on the fret-board the diagram is located. On the diagram you would play the 6th fret of the A string (which is the note of D♯).

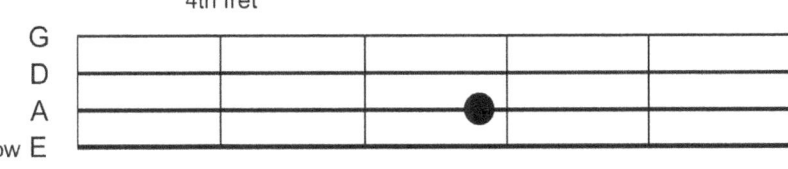

Sight-reading...a brief introduction

Although tablature is easy to understand and we can learn a piece of music from it relatively quickly, it doesn't tell us anything about rhythm. Conventional music notation on the other hand tells us about both pitch *and* rhythm. This is a basic introduction to notation so at this stage you don't have to sight-read. Later on in the book (page 50) the rhythmical aspect of notation will be covered so that you can use it in conjunction with tablature.

Conventional music notation is written on the five line *Staff* and is often included above tablature. In the example below, the notation and tablature both represent the same Bass guitar part. Both the staff and tablature are divided into bars, which are separated by bar lines.

Bass guitar music is written in the *Bass* clef which is at the start of the staff. The numbers just to the right of the clef, one on top of the other, are the *time signature*, which tells us about the pulse of the music; i.e. how we would count it.

The five horizontal lines of the staff don't represent strings in the way that tablature does. They are like a chart that tells us the pitch of the notes. The higher the note is placed on the staff the higher in pitch it is, and the lower the note is placed the lower in pitch it is. When notes are so high or low that they go outside of the staff, *ledger lines* are used to extend the staff, such as on the 2nd and 3rd bars of the example.

Whether the stem of any note points upward or downward is simply to make the staff look neat depending where the note is placed. The higher the note the stem goes down such as on the first two bars of the example, while the lower the note the stem goes up such as on the last two notes of the example.

> **Note:** Although conventional notation will be included above further tablatures, you don't have to read from it until later on when it is further explained.

Plucking Techniques

So far we've had a look at what the fretting hand is doing. Now it's time to look more closely at what the plucking hand is doing. There are a number of plucking techniques on the Bass. We will look at Fingerstyle first, followed by using a plectrum.

Fingerstyle

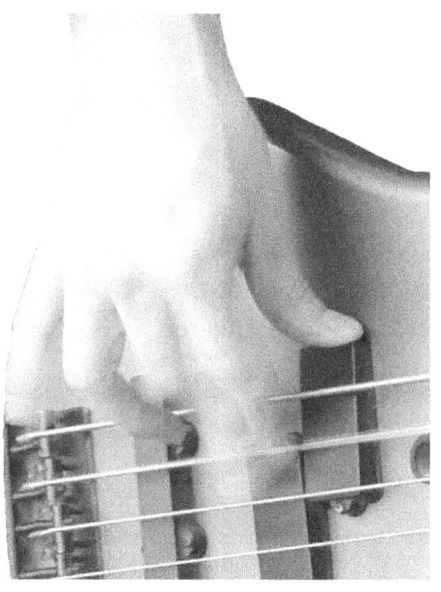

Fingerstyle is the most versatile and most often used. Rest your thumb on top of the pickup. Starting with the middle finger pluck the low E string and alternate between this and the index finger.

Although the index finger might feel more natural to start with it is *usually* better to lead with the middle finger because it is a bit longer therefore reaches the string and sits more naturally in place to start with. In the long run this will make for more consistent playing.

When playing the A, D or G strings you should rest the finger that has just plucked on the string below, so if plucking the A string the fingers are stopped by the E string. This is called the *rest stroke* and becomes useful if we need to move onto the string below, as will be explained shortly.

In the following exercise, as you move to pluck the higher strings the thumb needs to be flexible so that your hand can remain in the same posture, allowing your fingers to pluck the strings from the same angle. If the thumb remains too tense the fingers will be elevated from the higher strings when playing them. Notice that when changing strings the middle finger is the first to reach the next one up…

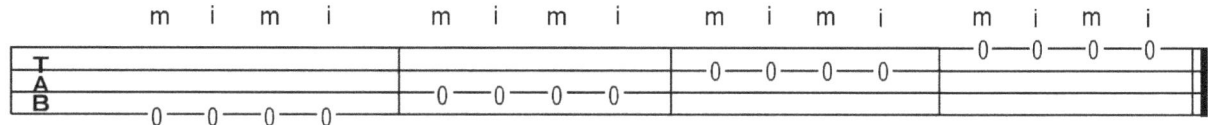

m = middle finger   i = index finger

> **Note:** When playing exercises like these it is strongly advised to use a metronome at a speed you can play consistently. Don't be impatient and rush.

Alternating between the middle and index finger offers more efficiency and potential speed, but when moving from a higher string to a lower one it is best to use the same finger. This is because the finger that was recently used to pluck the higher string falls naturally into position to play the one below (the rest stroke as explained on the previous page).

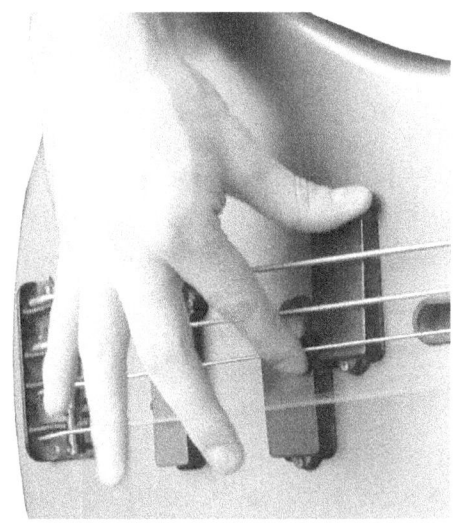

In the photo the index finger having just plucked the G string has fallen into place to play the D string, which it then plucks.

The following exercise descends from the G string to the low E string. Use the same finger when moving down a string…

```
        m   i   m   i       i   m   i   m       m   i   m   i       i   m   i   m
      0—0—0—0
T                       0—0—0—0
A
B                                             0—0—0—0
                                                                  0—0—0—0
```

You could join this with the previous exercise to go up and down through the strings…

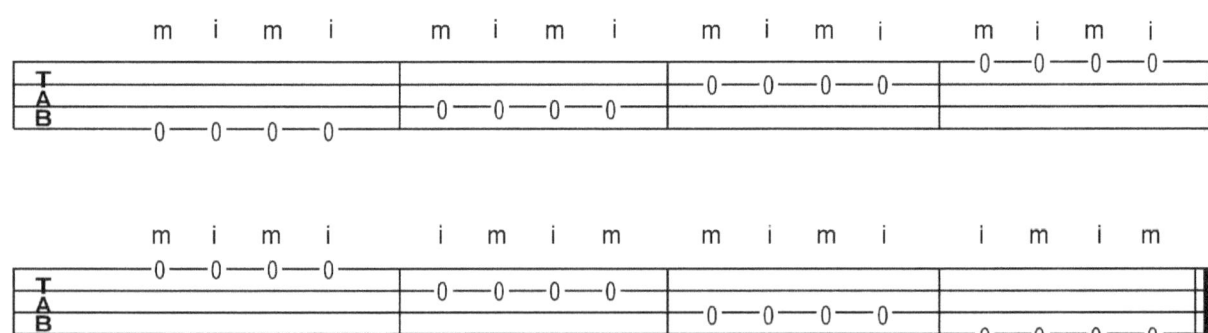

14

Plectrum

For the Bass guitar heavier plectrums are best because of the thicker strings. A thinner plectrum would be likely to flap about. The plectrum gives a harder sound compared to relatively softer fingers so is often used in heavier styles of music like Rock or Metal.

The pick should be held between the thumb and the index finger. The parts in contact with the pick should be the sole / tip area of the thumb and the side of the sole of the index finger. You could put your hand out in front of you and hold the pick as shown in the photo.

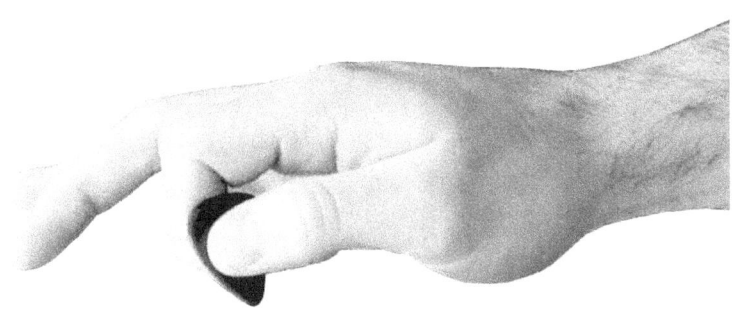

There shouldn't be too much pick sticking out from your grip. Too far out and we don't have as much control causing it to flap about within our grip as we pluck the strings.

When writing we hold the pen nearer the tip while resting the side of our hand on the paper, this way we can get control over the pen and write neatly. If we were to hold the pen further away from the tip without resting on the paper our writing could look pretty messy!

Similar applies to using a plectrum. It is best to rest your hand on the guitar, this way you can get more control and accurately play the strings you intend to…

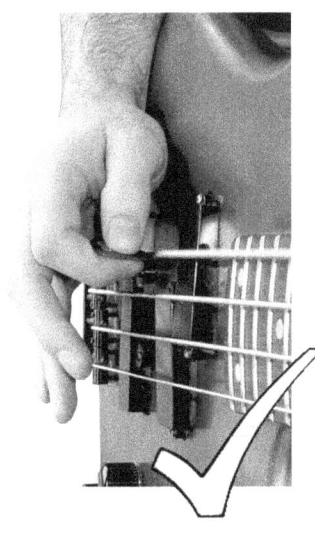

On the picture to the left the wrist / muscle at the base of the thumb area of the hand is resting on the Bass. Use this technique.

To the right the hand is hovering over the Bass. This isn't very easy to control and makes it more likely you will accidentally play strings that you didn't intend to.

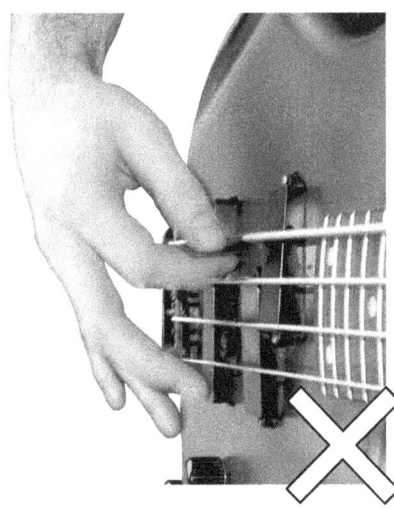

When playing the higher strings the hand moves down and the wrist / muscle at base of thumb area rests on the lower strings. This mutes the lower strings when we don't want them to sound. It also maintains the same posture for the hand across all four strings rather than bending the wrist down and stretching the fingers to reach the higher ones.

Some players like to have the remaining fingers tucked in, others like to have them fanned out.

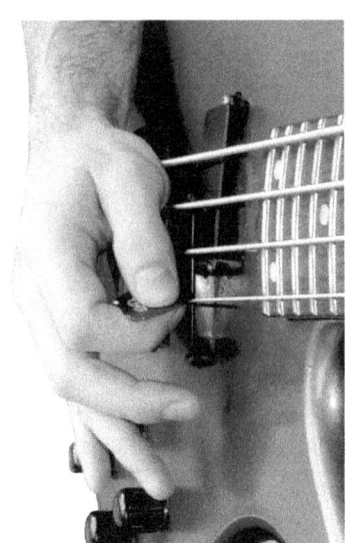

Alternate Picking

It can be tempting to do what feels natural and to some this might mean only picking with a downward motion. However in order to get to the next downward pick you have to move the plectrum back up to get into position anyway, so why not use this upward motion to pick as well and increase the efficiency and potential speed that you can play? Let's start by picking the A string down and up to give a repeating A note. This is best done to a metronome so that you can practise getting an even tempo…

Down **Up**

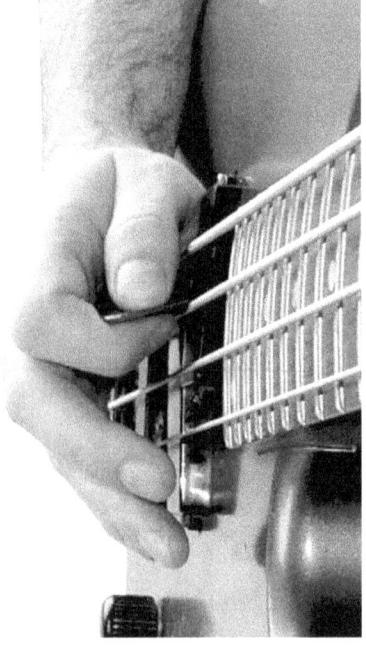 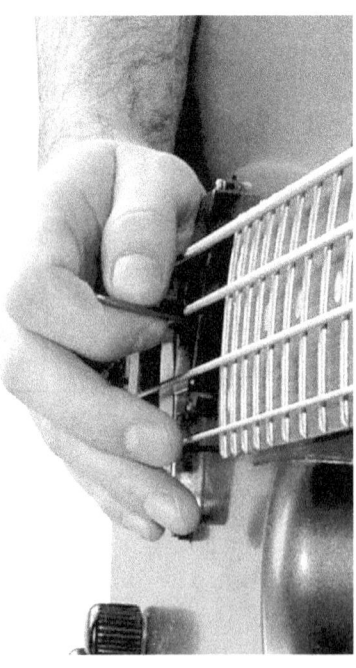

For the thick strings of the Bass guitar the pick should be held firmly.

However it needs to tilt very slightly within your grip as it rolls off the string. The pictures to the left exaggerate to show this. In practise the angle is more discreet.

In situations where speed is required, the pick can be rotated forward slightly so its curved tip rolls off the strings (similar to the picture top right of this page).

Below is an exercise for alternate picking that goes through all four strings.

The arches ⊓ and points V represent downward and upward pick strokes. Arches for downward and points for upward. As you move up and down the strings try to maintain the same posture in the hand (as mentioned at the top of the last page)…

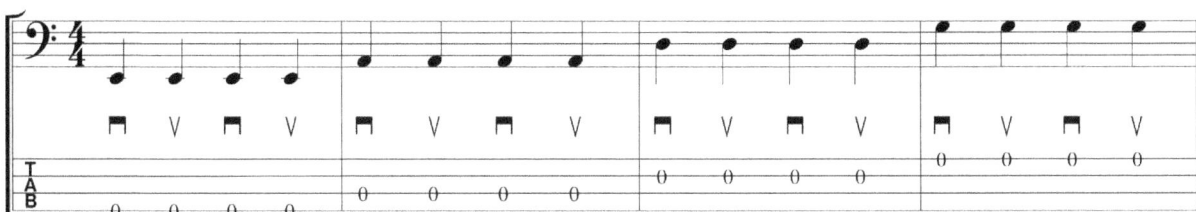

If the arches and points don't seem to make sense, it might be worth noting that these symbols originate from the different ends of a violin bow. The arch is for the blunt end near where the bow is held which moves towards the floor when pulling the bow down. The point is for the pointed end of the bow, which moves upwards when pushing the bow up. Seeing as the downward motions are usually on a stronger beat, it might help to remember it by how the arch is more substantial and blocky looking.

Fretting Hand Technique

So far we've only used the fretting hand for the tutorial on tablature, now let's look a bit further into fretting hand technique before we continue.

Photos **1** and **2** show good position for the fretting hand. The four fingers are spread out on the frets while the thumb behind the neck is roughly central to the opposing fingers. The only parts of the hand that should be in contact with the guitar are the fingertips on the fret-board, and the "pad" of the thumb behind on the neck. This posture also makes it easier to shift up and down the neck…

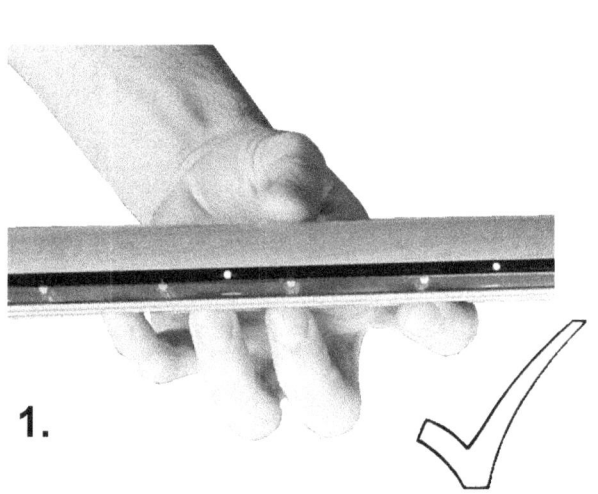

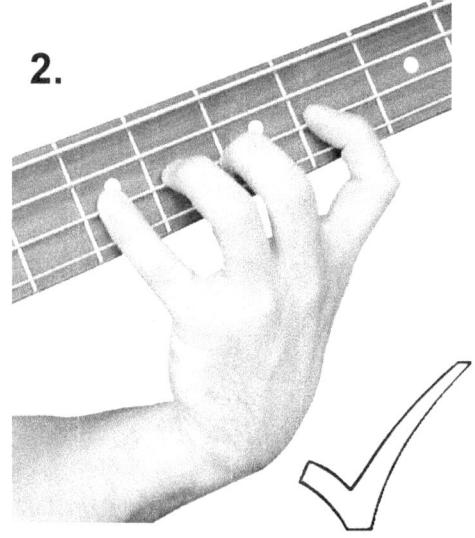

On lower frets of the Bass, four frets across is just about the width that the four fingers can stretch (this will be easier further up the fret-board where the frets are closer together). Due to the distance of the frets on the Bass you may sometimes need to move the hand a little while in the same position on the fret-board.

Photos **3** and **4** (4 over the page) demonstrate bad technique. In 3 the palm is hugging the bottom of the neck while the thumb is over the top. The fingers are too close to the fret-board to manoeuvre and the hand can't move up and down the neck very easily. The fingers will also have to bend back toward the palm in order to fret the higher strings.

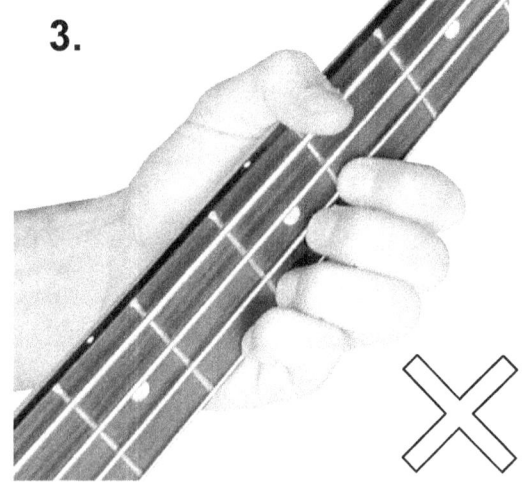

There are exceptions to the "thumb / hug" position. Putting the thumb over the top can offer extra support for parts which are tricky and need more stamina / strength.

In photo 4 the thumb isn't positioned centrally to the fingers as it rests behind the neck. Instead it is resting flat and is past the index finger, making it harder for the 3rd and the little finger to reach higher frets.

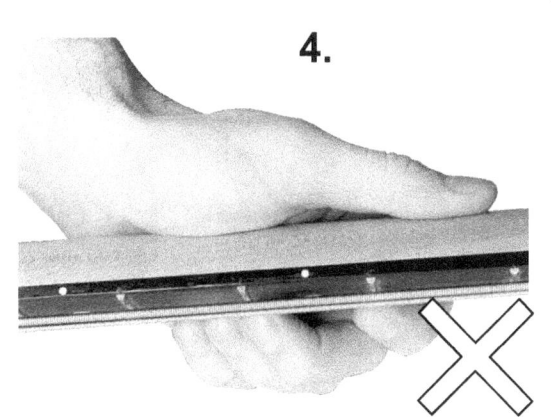

Poor technique can be due to the hand having not developed enough strength and shouldn't become a habit.

With classical guitar technique the neck is tilted even further upwards bringing the neck a bit closer making it easier for the wrist angle. Basically you rest the guitar on the inner leg rather than atop the leg. A foot-stand for the supporting leg can help.

Considering that the Bass guitar's neck is fairly long there's no reason not to practise it (and other types of guitar) with the classical position if it's more comfortable.

The following Bass line has numbers underneath to help with the rhythm. The ones circled in black are when the notes occur...

E Major Blues

A Bass line should be "tight" which means the notes are right where they should be on whichever beats they fall on. A simple Bass line played to a high standard is far better than a more complex or faster one that isn't played tight.

That's the end of the first chapter here are a few questions…

1. When fretting a note, where in relation to the fret should your finger push down?

2. Why is tablature "upside down"?

3. What does conventional music notation indicate that tablature doesn't?

4. When plucking with finger style, where should the thumb of your plucking-hand be?

5. Which finger should you usually lead with and why?

6. Normally you would alternate between the middle and index finger but when is it best to use the same finger?

7. When playing with a plectrum should your arm hover above the Bass as you play or should you rest the wrist / muscle at the base of the thumb area on the Bass?

8. For the fretting hand, where behind the neck should the thumb be placed?

(You will find the answers at the back of the book)

2 Fundamentals

Fret-board Layout

There are twelve notes in music, as follows…

1	2	3	4	5	6	7	8	9	10	11	12
A	A♯/B♭	B	C	C♯/D♭	D	D♯/E♭	E	F	F♯/G♭	G	G♯/A♭

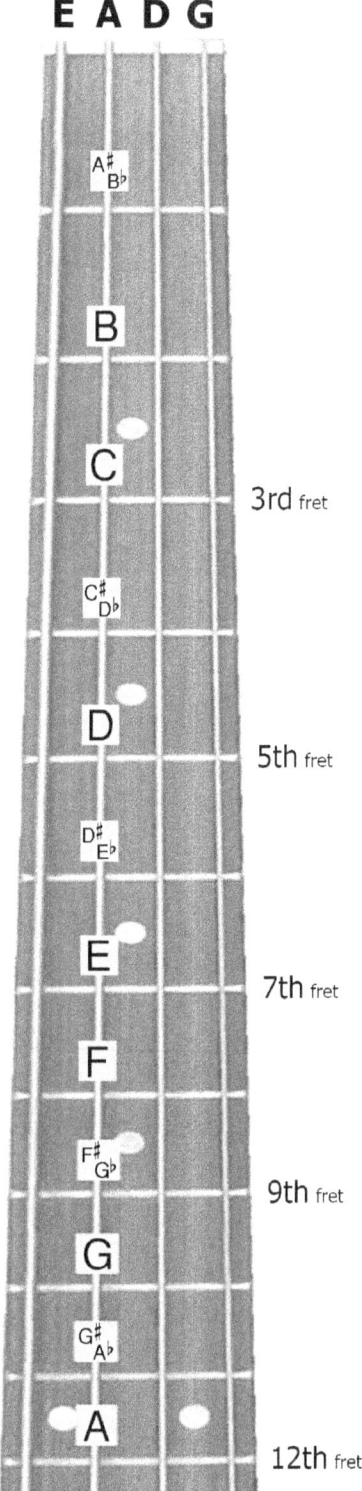

The diagram to the right shows how the notes are arranged across the A string as they go up its frets. At the 12th fret we return to the note of A but at a higher pitch, this is known as an *octave.* If we were to continue above the 12th fret to the 13th and upward, the notes would repeat in a higher octave A♯/B♭, B, C etc…

Like the chart we can see that B and C are next to each other as are E and F. All of the other notes are two frets apart with a flat or sharp note in between (signified with ♯ for sharp and ♭ for flat). These are different names for the same note, also known as *enharmonic equivalents*.

This is similar to how the keys of a piano are laid out. Below is a diagram that shows a section of the piano. The notes go across the keys in a linear fashion similar to a single string of the guitar. There are also octaves on the piano, so if you go up (or down) the keys eventually you end up on the same note but at a higher (or lower) pitch. A couple are marked out on the diagram…

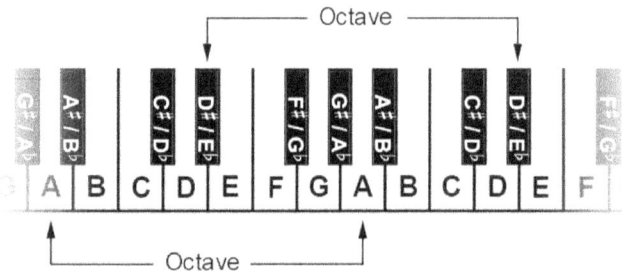

The Bass guitar has four strings however! Over the page, another diagram shows the notes of all four strings of the Bass up to the 12th fret…

Before we go any further, it's worth pointing out that the idea of this section is to learn how the fret-board is laid out. You're not expected to learn all the notes at this stage.

Starting with the note of the open string, the musical alphabet goes up the frets of each of the strings until at the 12th fret it reaches the higher octave. For example the D string starts on D and goes up the musical alphabet until on the 12th fret it reaches the note of D again in a higher octave.

The notes occur several times over all four strings. For example the note of E occurs on the…

Open low E string and its 12th fret

A string 7th fret

D string 2nd fret

G string 9th fret

If you play those and listen while comparing you'll hear that 12th fret low E string, 7th fret A string and 2nd fret D string are the same, while G string 9th fret is in a higher octave and low E string open is the lowest octave. This may seem complex at first but there are advantages to the layout of the fret-board such as transposing shapes by the root note (explained later).

The human ear is tuned in to mid range frequencies (600Hz – 1.5Khz) and less sensitive to bass frequencies. To the human ear chords on the Bass would sound muddy with the notes blending into each other. The Bass guitar takes care of the low end of the frequency range of the band. It's part of the rhythm section somewhere between drums and rhythm guitar. It keeps the beat but it's melodic at the same time. For these reasons Bass lines are often made of notes from chords played separately. Known as *Arpeggios*.

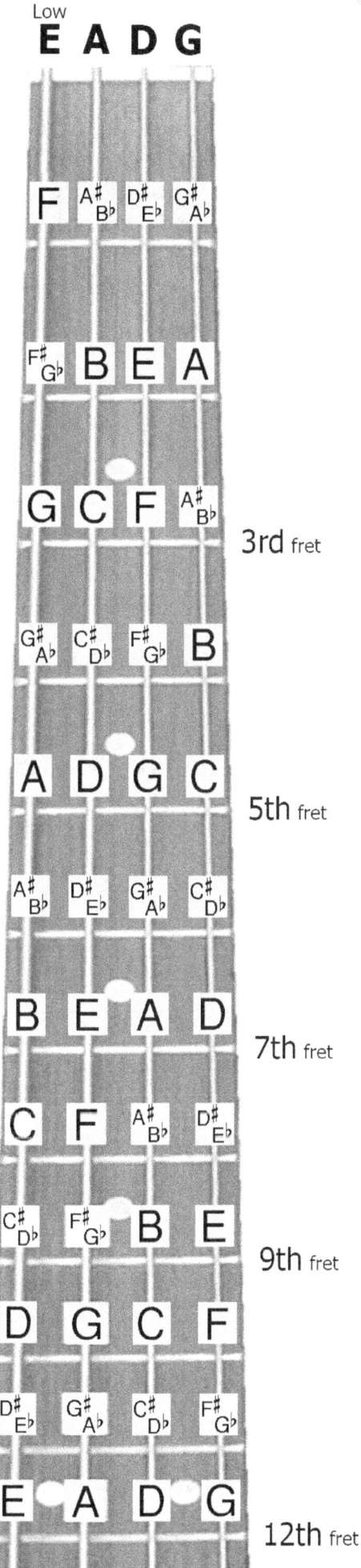

Creating Bass Lines

The first, simplest way of doing this is by playing the root note of the chord. A chord's root note is the note letter you see in the beginning of its name, for example the root note of a G major chord will be the note of G, the root note of a G minor chord (Gm) will be also be the note of G. No matter how complex, all chords have a root note; the root note of a D♭minor7#5♭9 chord is simply the note of D♭ (D flat). The following Bass line uses the root note of each chord. You could check what the notes are on the fret-board diagram from the previous page…

Roots

(Explanation of this symbol on next page)

This is a repeat sign. When you get to it, go back to the beginning then straight through again to the end…

Although perhaps technically simple to play, the Bass line is a guide for you to develop an awareness of what the notes are rather than simply going through tablature. For a Bassist to be able to make Bass lines in this way it is important to learn the note names on the fret-board.

You don't have to stick to what has been written you could make up your own rhythm, as long as you are aware that these are the root notes of the corresponding chords written above. The same applies to all of the arpeggio pieces in the book; the simple Bass-lines are a guide for the notes from within the chords.

As was explained earlier on page 22 an *octave* is the same note but in a higher or lower pitch. For any note on the low E or A string, an octave higher can be found two strings and two frets up, as the following two examples show…

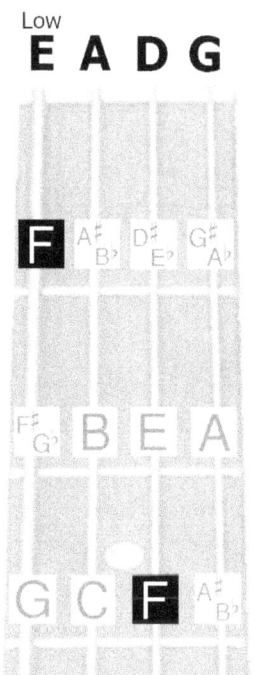

…To the left the note of F and it's higher octave have been highlighted.

To the right, the 2nd finger is playing the higher octave of the open A string…

Over the page is a Bass line that uses roots and their higher octaves. As before you can follow the Tab while being aware these are the root notes of the chords and you can confirm what the notes are on the fret-board diagram.

The piece has a corresponding repeat sign facing the other way (on bar 9). This indicates where the repeat is to begin, so after the repeat symbol at the end of bar 12, rather than going back to the beginning, go back to bar 9 then continue from there to the end…

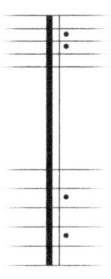

25

Roots and Octaves  5 & 6

Playing the root notes of the chords doesn't only apply to these exercises you can use the same process for any song that has the chords written out. So if you have the chords for any of your favourite songs you could make a simple Bass-line.

The Structure of Music

Now that we have looked at playing the root notes of chords, it's time to start looking at the structure of music so that we can eventually play other notes from the chords.

In Western music there are two fundamental distances between notes, these are the *Tone* and the *Semitone*. On the Bass guitar (and guitar) a tone is two frets apart while a semitone is one fret apart, both can be in either direction back or forth...

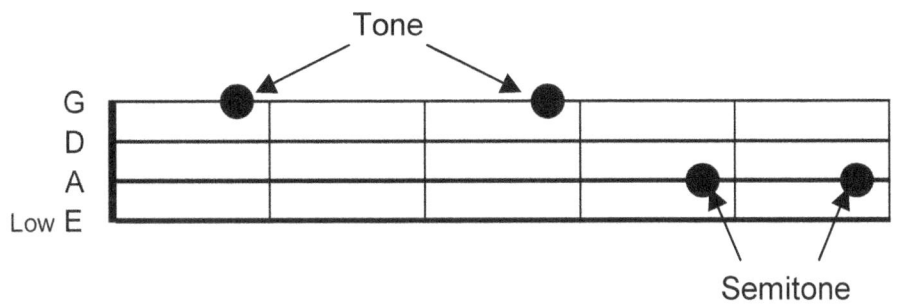

It doesn't matter where you are on the fret-board tone and semitone, are always the same.

Sequences of tones and semitones are used to make scales, and the first and most important scale we'll be looking at is the Major scale.

The Major Scale

The Major scale is the basis of music in the West. Everything else in Western music is defined in comparison to it. Scales may seem boring at first but knowing them, particularly this one, opens up doorways to understanding many other aspects of music. The Major scale consists of seven notes, their distance from each other measured in tones and semitones. This gives us numbers known as *intervals,* which relate to how far the notes are from starting note (the root). As follows...

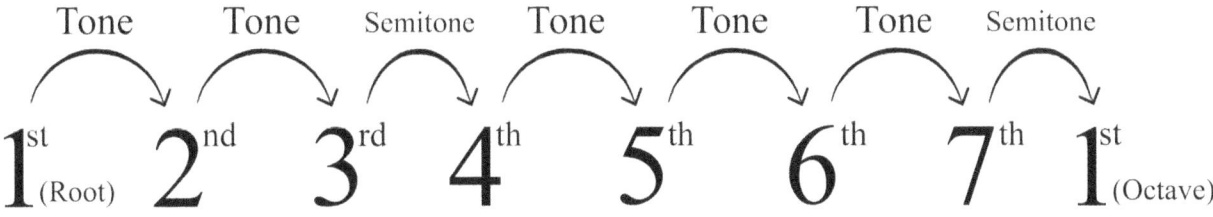

The formula takes us to the higher octave of the root note (all scales span an octave, what scale it is depends on the sroute between). An easier way to remember the Major scale is that there are tones between all of the intervals except between the 3rd and 4th and between the 7th and the octave, which have a semitone between them.

The full names for these intervals are the *major 2nd, major 3rd, perfect 4th, perfect 5th, major 6th and major 7th*. The 4th and 5th are known as *perfect* because they are neither major nor minor. Scales are usually indicated with numbers like the previous diagram, so the Major scale could be represented simply as 1 2 3 4 5 6 7.

Let's create a Major scale on the Bass. Start with the 1st fret of the D string giving us the note of E♭. This will be the root note of our Major scale. From this root note, move up the fret board according to the formula **TTSTTTS** and we should end up with a completed Major scale…

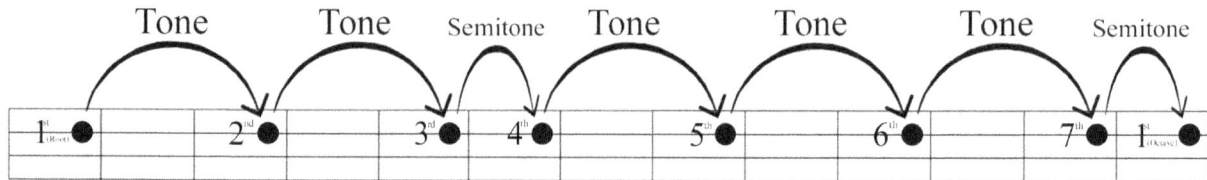

You have just created an E♭ major scale. This formula will work from anywhere, so we can create any Major scale by choosing the root note then applying the formula. We can call this *transposing by the root note*. Remember after the 12th fret the notes repeat themselves in a higher octave. Why not make some other Major scales?

Using the fret-board diagram we can see what the notes are of any Major scale that we make. On the next page D major is highlighted.

> **Note:** The Tone and Semitone can also be referred to as the "Wholetone" and "Halftone" but it's easier to say TTSTTTS (and therefore perhaps remember) than WWHWWWH.

The notes of the D major scale are…

D E F♯ G A B C♯ D

The reason two of the notes are known as sharps instead of flats, is because this keeps it alphabetical. If we had called those notes flats then the letters G and D would both have occurred twice as G♭ then G and D♭ then D.

Why not work some out for yourself using the diagram? Choose a root note near the nut then work your way up the frets of the string according to the Major scale formula.

If you start on the 1st fret of the low E string to give us an F major scale, is the 4th interval (on the 6th fret) best known as B flat or A sharp?

What are the notes of a G major scale?

What are the notes of the E♭ major scale from earlier and are the notes that fall on enharmonic equivalents better known as sharps or flats?

~

The major scale across one string gives a visual representation of how far the notes are from each other and is similar to the way the scale would be played across the keys of a piano. However, so that we don't have to move up and down the Bass guitar's neck, versions that go across different strings should be learnt, of which there are three. This will be covered shortly in a section called "Fundamental Major Scale Shapes".

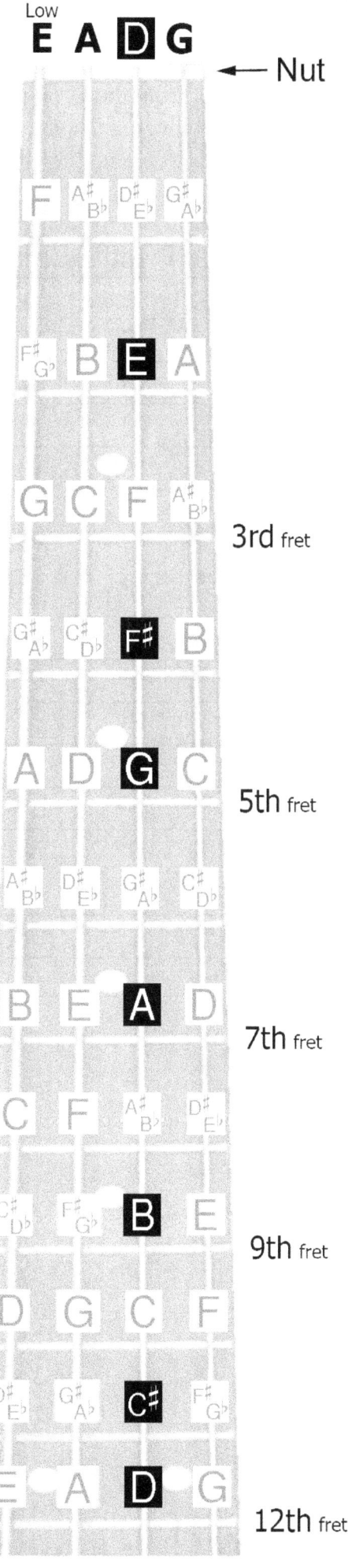

Often music is based on the major scale i.e. the notes of a song are from it. This is known as being in a *Major key* so for example a piece of music in the key of G major will use notes from the G major scale. Here is a chart of all the major scales / keys and their notes (you could use it the check your answers for the previous page)...

Major key	1st (Root)	2nd	3rd	4th	5th	6th	7th	1st (Octave)
C major	C	D	E	F	G	A	B	C
G major	G	A	B	C	D	E	F♯	G
D major	D	E	F♯	G	A	B	C♯	D
A major	A	B	C♯	D	E	F♯	G♯	A
E major	E	F♯	G♯	A	B	C♯	D♯	E
B major	B	C♯	D♯	E	F♯	G♯	A♯	B
F♯ major	F♯	G♯	A♯	B	C♯	D♯	E♯	F♯
C♯ major	C♯	D♯	E♯	F♯	G♯	A♯	B♯	C♯
F major	F	G	A	B♭	C	D	E	F
B♭ major	B♭	C	D	E♭	F	G	A	B♭
E♭ major	E♭	F	G	A♭	B♭	C	D	E♭
A♭ major	A♭	B♭	C	D♭	E♭	F	G	A♭
D♭ major	D♭	E♭	F	G♭	A♭	B♭	C	D♭
G♭ major	G♭	A♭	B♭	C♭	D♭	E♭	F	G♭
C♭ major	C♭	D♭	E♭	F♭	G♭	A♭	B♭	C♭

The concept of keys will be looked at in more detail further on in the book.

Fretting Exercise

Before we continue with more complex fingering let's look at some exercises for finger coordination. It can be tempting to use only the strongest fingers on the fret-board. However, if we learn to use all of the fingers we can play more efficiently and potentially faster.

The following exercises train each finger to move independently. They should be done to a metronome so that you can develop consistency in your technique and a sense of timing. Start slowly. On the next page is some advice on technique (Minimising Movement) feel free to browse it before starting. Go back and forth between the pairs of fingers while plucking by alternating between the middle and index finger or use alternate picking if you prefer to use a plectrum…

1st and 2nd finger…

1st and 3rd finger…

1st and 4th finger…

2nd and 3rd finger…

2nd and 4th finger…

3rd and 4th finger…

Although the 3rd and 4th fingers have different tendons they are connected to the same muscle in the forearm. Independence between them may need some practise.

If we put them all together we get the following…

Here it is played backwards, you might find this trickier…

The exercises are placed with the first finger on the 5th fret D string but you could play the "12121313 etc" finger pattern (and backwards) anywhere on the fret-board.

Minimising Movement

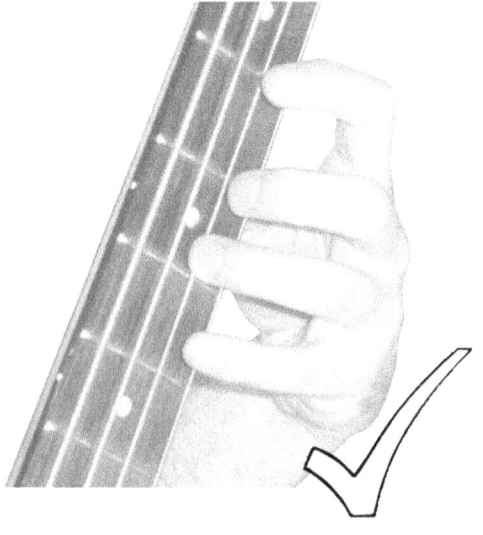

In the photo to the left the fingers are kept close to the fret-board. This way less movement is needed when changing between them. Try to keep the fingers near the fret-board like this when they are not in use.

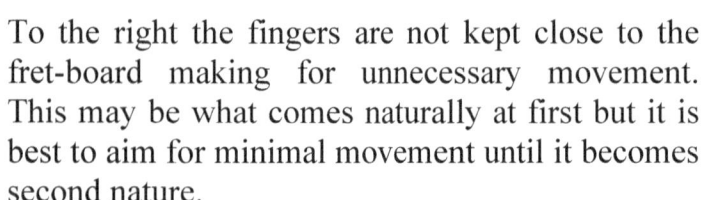

To the right the fingers are not kept close to the fret-board making for unnecessary movement. This may be what comes naturally at first but it is best to aim for minimal movement until it becomes second nature.

If you have trouble getting the correct technique (e.g. if any of your fretting fingers push against each other and aren't independent as you play), you could try moderately tensing the hand and fingers and playing very slow. Doing this will mean all the muscles are activated *including* the ones that are actually needed but that you can't yet activate on their own.

With practise the brain learns to keep the muscles that are needed active while switching off the ones that aren't. Eventually it should start to feel more natural. This technique can be effective but stop if it starts to feel a strain.

Here is a finger exercise that goes across all six strings. Use fingers 1 2 3 4 on the way up and 4 3 2 1 on the way down…

You could make up your own finger patterns using any combination of fingers 1, 2, 3 and 4. For example 1 2 4 3 on the way up the strings, then 4 3 1 2 on the way down or 1 4 2 3 on the way up then 4 1 3 2 on the way down. Tough at first but variation can prepare us for whatever may be in music and don't forget you can play these exercises starting from any fret.

These exercises reflect how generally when playing you should span your fingers across the frets. It was originally mentioned on "Fretting Hand Technique" (page 18 pictures 1 and 2) that you should spread your fingers out across the frets.

~

As mentioned earlier on page 29 the major scale across a single string gives a visual representation of how far the notes are from each other. The next section shows how to play it across different strings so that we can keep the hand in the same position…

33

Fundamental Major Scale Shapes

Below, a C major scale is arranged across different strings in three different shapes named according to their relative positions to each other on the fret-board. The Low shape has two versions depending where you play the 7th interval. C major is used here to show that they share the same notes therefore are the same scale, but the most important way to learn these is by their generic intervals (as shown over the page)…

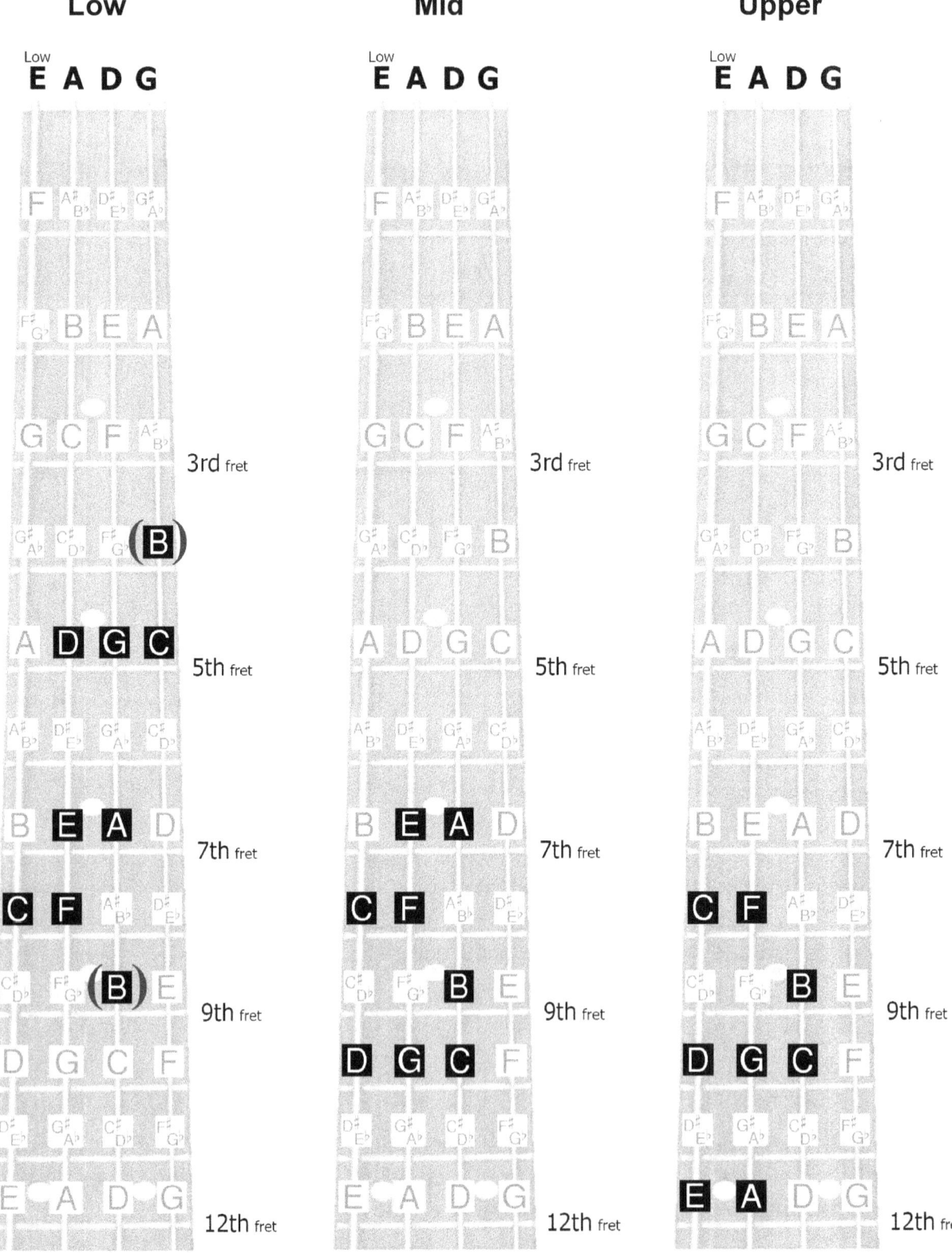

Here they are with their generic intervals; R = root, 2 = 2nd etc (over the page they are also in tablature with finger numbers to help with how to play them). A useful way of identifying these is by how many notes they have on the string that the root is on, including the root itself.

Low

Has <u>one</u> note on the roots string (the root note itself)…

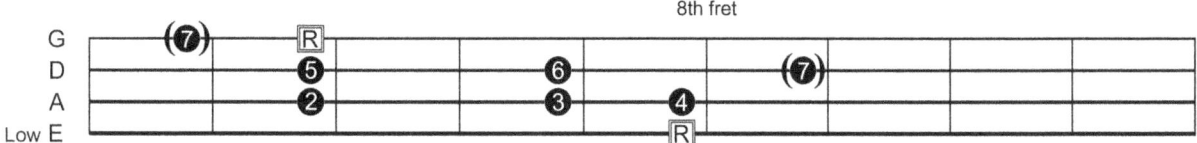

Mid

Has <u>two</u> notes on the roots string…

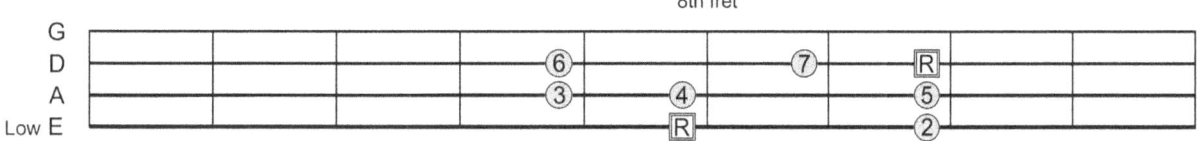

Upper

Has <u>three</u> notes on the roots string…

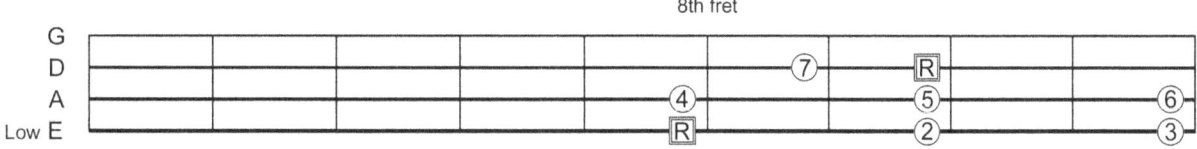

These three "Low, Mid and Upper" shapes aren't "*official*" but they make learning the fret-board easier by categorising the all important major scale into just three shapes which offer a grounding upon which the fret-board can be understood further.

Low

or...

Mid

Upper

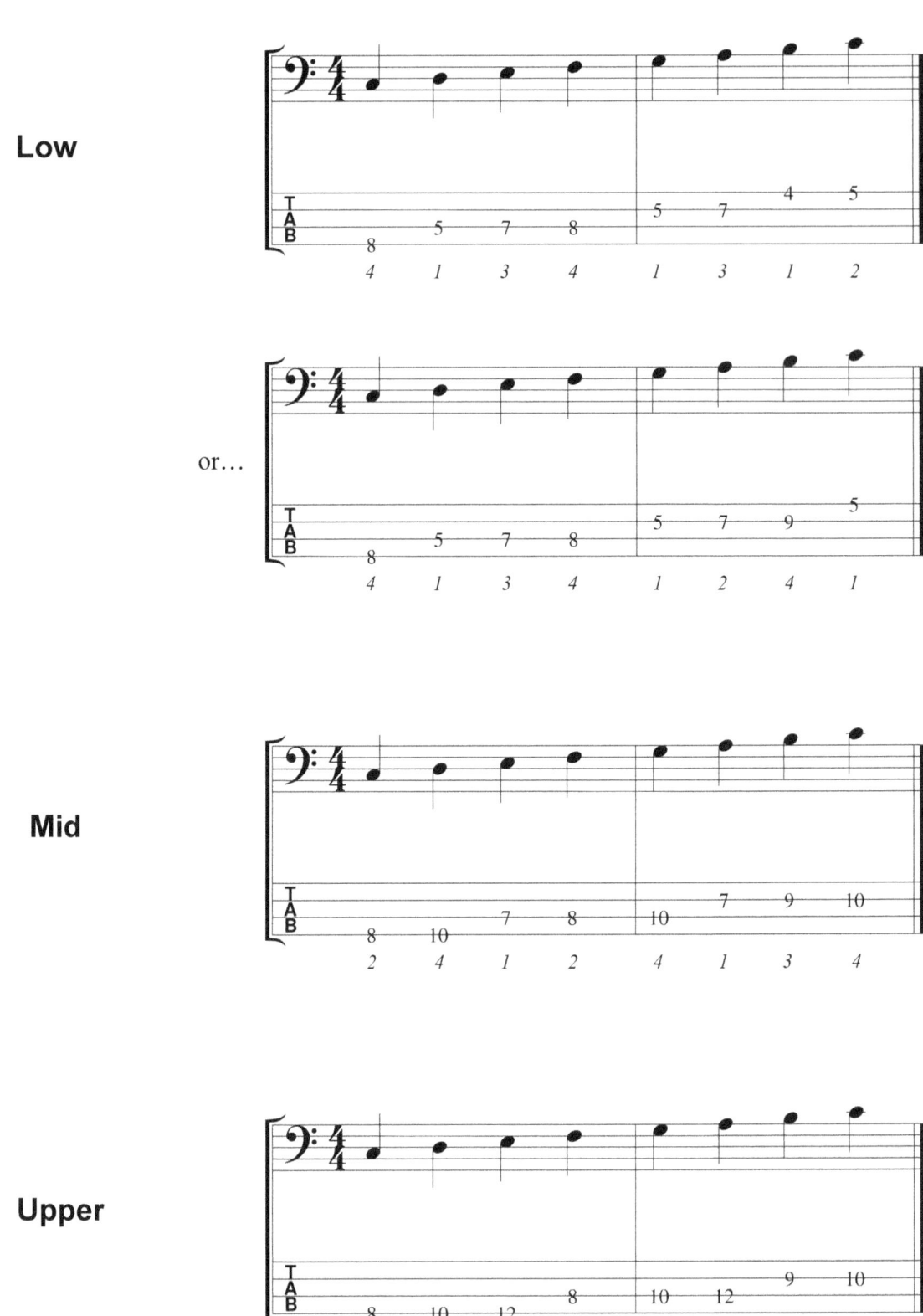

Note: When there are two frets up followed by another two frets up on the same string; it's easier to use the 1st, 2nd then 4th fingers rather than 1st, 3rd then 4th because two frets is quite a stretch between the 3rd and 4th finger.

Learn these one at a time if you prefer starting with Mid. Practise them forwards and backwards.

Transposing by the root note

When we created the major scale across a single string (on page 28) we could start from any note for the root then apply the **TTSTTTS** formula up the string giving us different major scales (such as C major if starting on C, or F major if starting on F etc).

This principle doesn't only apply to the single-string major scale in fact it applies to anything on the fret-board. *Transposing by the root note* means shifting a shape elsewhere so that it starts on a different root note.

To demonstrate this we will use the three fundamental major scale shapes and move them around from the C major that was originally used to show them (on page 34). On the diagram to the right, the Low shape has been moved down by three frets making its root note A therefore it's now an A major scale (the notes for this and the following two examples can be confirmed from the chart on page 30).

Over the page are a couple more examples using the other two fundamental major scale shapes.

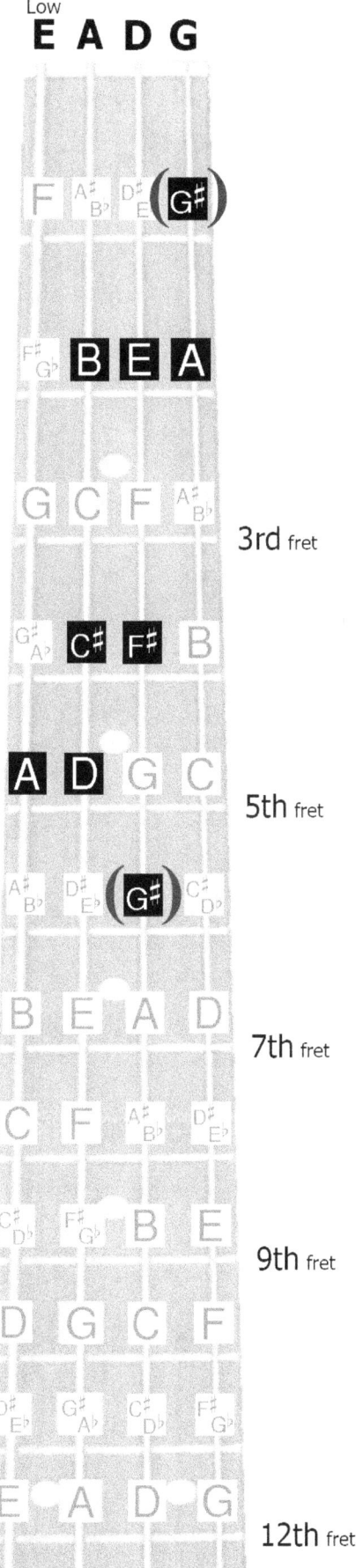

On the left the Mid shape has been shifted up a string making its root note F therefore it's now an F major scale. To the right the Upper shape has been moved down three frets *and* shifted up a string making its root note D therefore now it is D major…

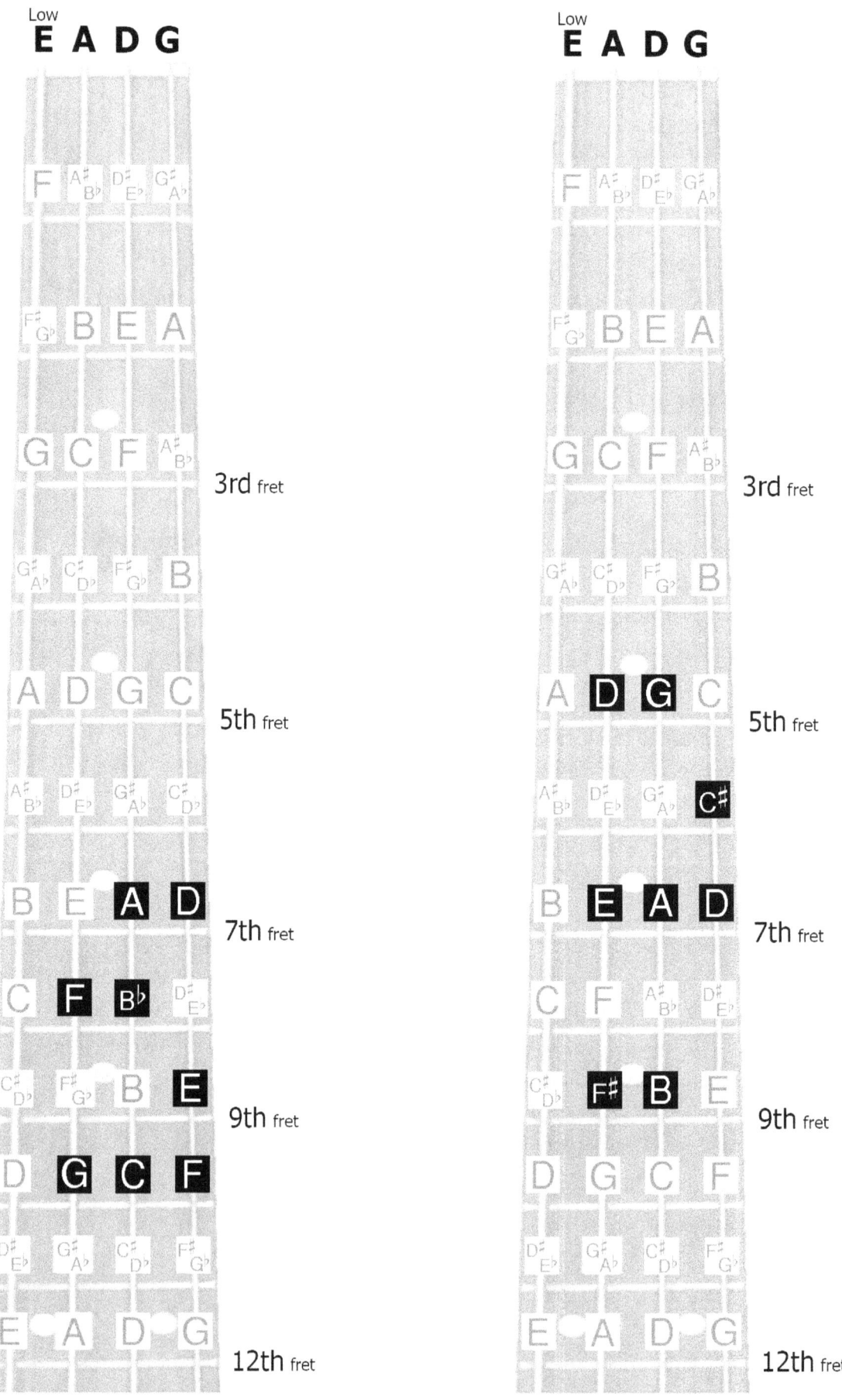

Arpeggios

Now that we've looked at the major scale and how the fret-board works, let's look at the structure of chords and therefore the arpeggios that we can use with them on the Bass (as mentioned at the bottom of page 23 an arpeggio is the notes of a chord played separately).

Major Triad

At the first and most basic level chords are made by using odd numbered intervals from a scale. The first kind of chord we will be looking at is the major triad, consisting of the **Root, 3rd** and **5th**. Here are three shapes for the major triad played as arpeggios on the Bass, taken from the fundamental major scale shapes…

> **Note:** The arpeggio shapes in this book are shown with their root note on no particular fret as they will work anywhere on the fret-board (i.e. they can be transposed by the root note).

Low

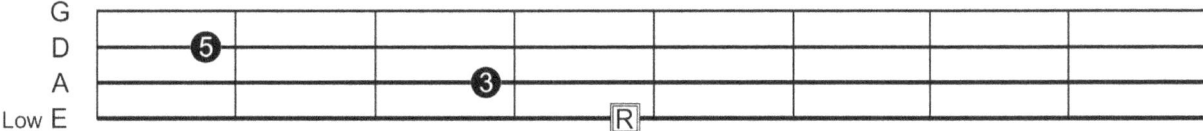

Mid

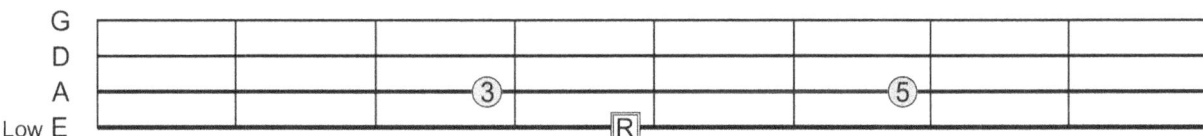

Upper

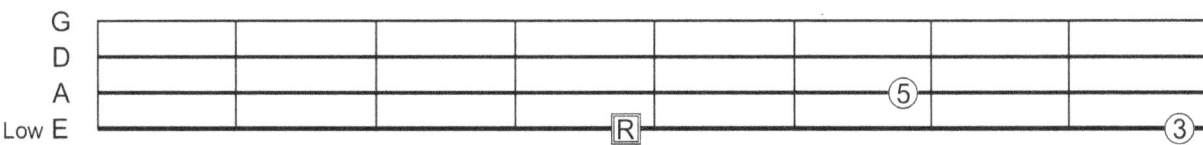

The major triad from the Upper spans one fret more than the other two so is therefore more of a stretch and tougher to play, but can be useful for when the root note is on an open string.

Minor Triad

Another kind of chord is the minor triad in which the 3rd is lowered by a semitone (one fret) giving us a *minor 3rd* so consisting of the **Root, minor 3rd** and **5th**. This semitone lowering is indicated with the use of the flat symbol ♭ (this is different from note names such as "G♭ or E♭" so don't get them confused). Here are three shapes for the minor triad played as arpeggios, taken from the fundamental major scale shapes (with the 3rd lowered)…

Low

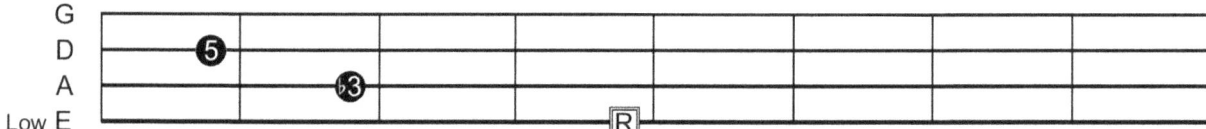

Mid

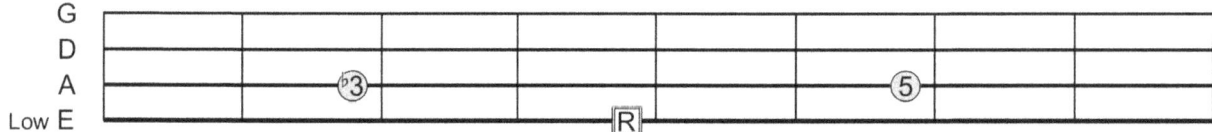

Upper

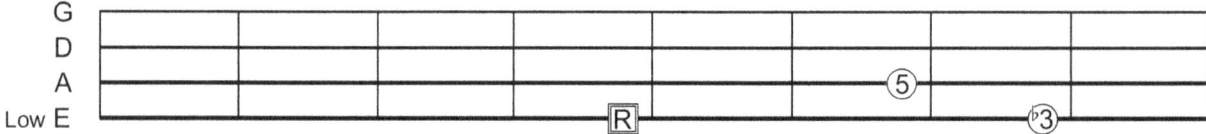

The minor triad from the Mid is the most difficult as it spans more frets than the other two.

Don't forget that transposing by the root note applies to anything so these shapes can be moved around. Here's a B minor arpeggio with its root note on the 2nd fret of the A string…

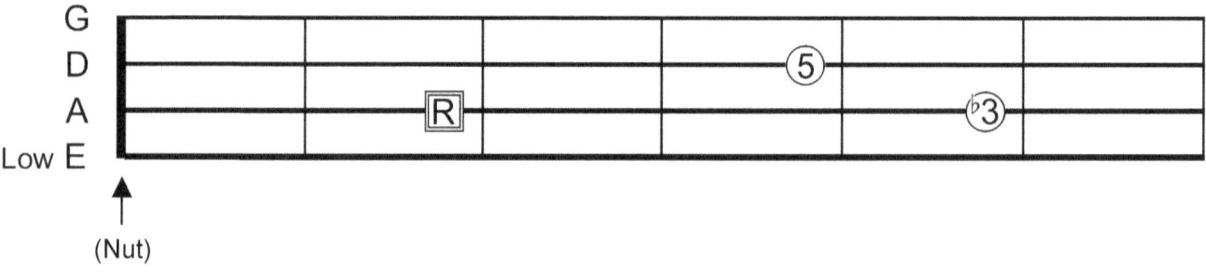

As major and minor arpeggios both have the interval of the perfect 5th in common, we could play only the roots and 5ths over a chord sequence that contains both major and minor chords. This is a valid and sometimes desired approach. The Bass line for the song "Lyin' Eyes" by the Eagles uses mostly roots and 5ths quite aptly, so does "Hotel California". Here is a Bass line using only roots and 5ths over major and minor chords…

There is a type of simplified chord containing only the Root and 5th known as a "Power chord" indicated with the number 5 after the root note, often used in heavier styles of music like Rock. In the following Bass line for the arpeggios over the C5 and G5 chords the location of the 5th is where it would be from within the *low* shape. The rhythm is slightly different now too, with the root on beats **1** and **3** of the first bar then the 5th played on the beats **1, 2** and **3** of the next...

Next we have a Bossa style piece with a Bass line that uses only the root and 5th over major and minor chords. Sometimes the arpeggios here use the higher octave of the root note also.

The rhythm for the beats is split with an *and* in between (represented by +). You would count this "**One** and two **and** three and four and". The repeat section is played three times for this piece…

Bossa Bassa 11 & 12

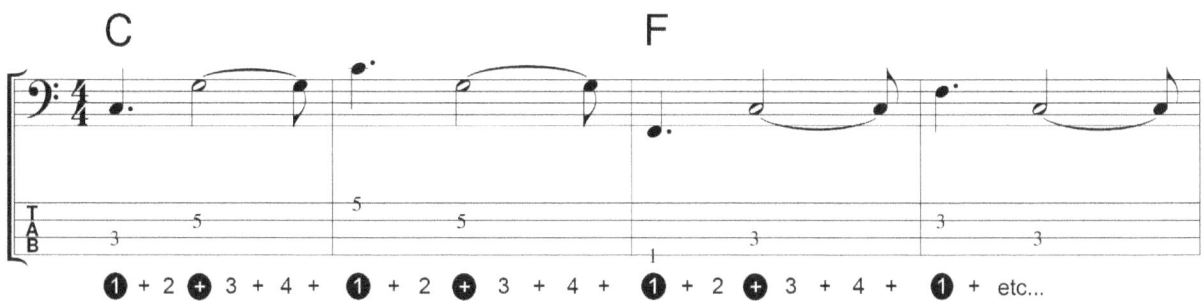

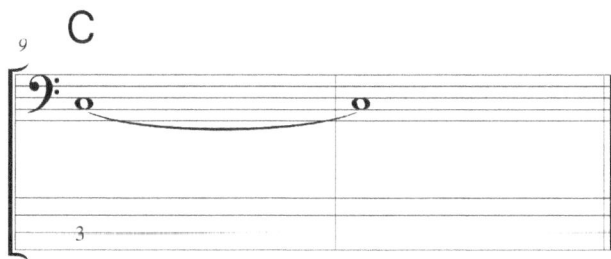

Now let's start using 3rds as well. The Bass line for the Bluesy Jazz track on the next page uses major arpeggios over major chords. Some of the arpeggios are from the Upper shape as their root notes are on open strings (this was mentioned earlier on page 39).

43

Major Arpeggios

In music the intervals for the arpeggios don't necessarily have to start on the root or be in the order of Root, 3rd then 5th. In the above piece the sequence of intervals over the C major chord on bars 3 - 4 (and on bars 15 - 16) is 5th, 3rd, Root then 3rd.

Here's a Bass line using minor arpeggios over minor chords. This piece has a first and second ending; Play to the repeat sign at the end of bar 4 and repeat from the start, but this time around, after the 2nd bar jump to the 5th bar on the next line and continue the piece from there to the end…

Minor Arpeggios

Now for a Bass line that uses both major and minor arpeggios over major and minor chords…

Major and Minor Arpeggios 🎵 17 & 18

Developing Plucking technique

Following are two pieces to develop co-ordination in your plucking hand. **m** and **i** are indicated as a suggested pattern for finger style, while arches and points are also included if you use a plectrum. This piece uses a first and second ending...

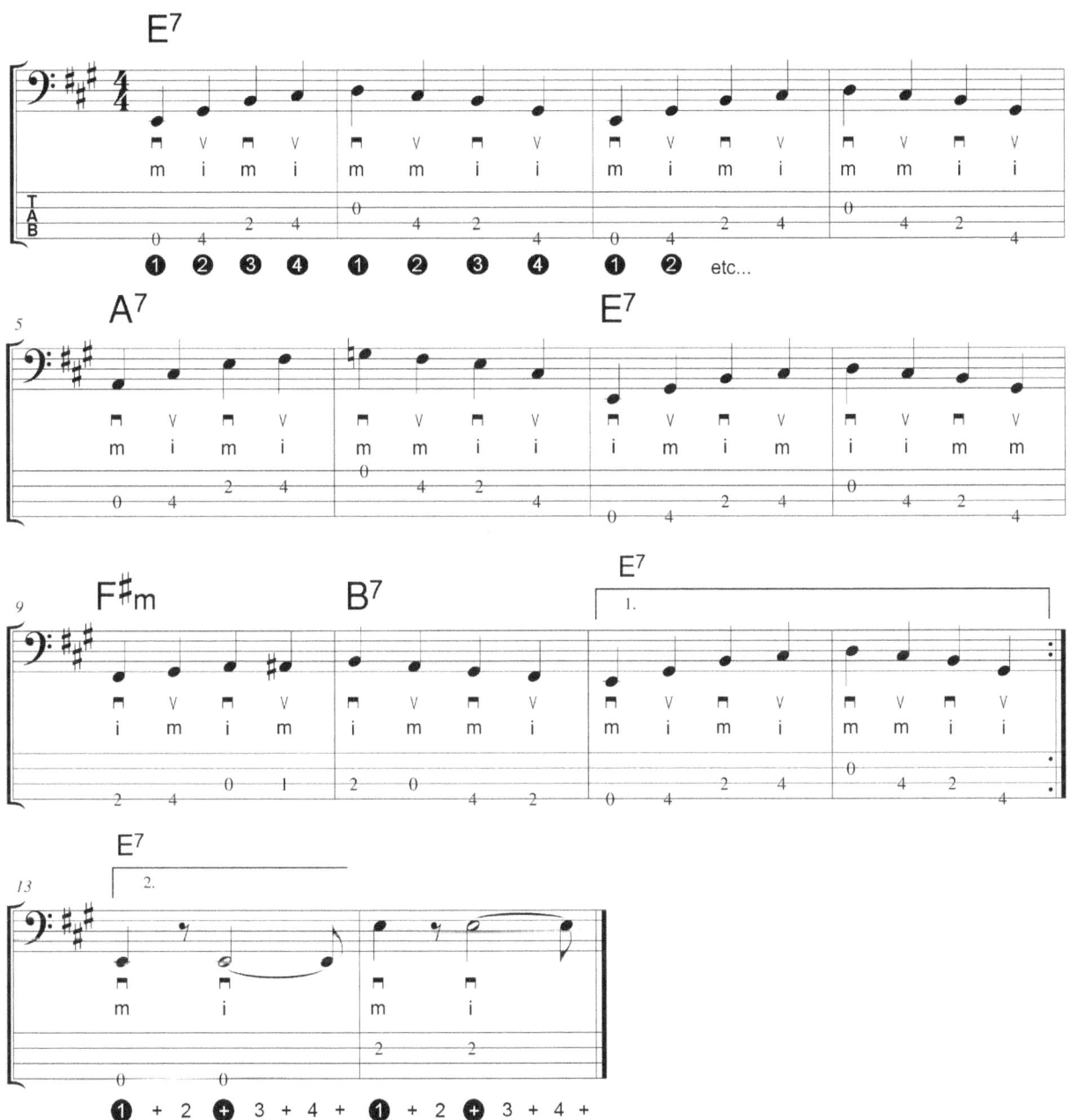

This piece is started with the index finger. This is because the next note is on the A string and the middle finger has a better reach, while on the next bar the slightly shorter index finger moves back easier across the strings to the low E to repeat the same phrase. No repeats, one time through…

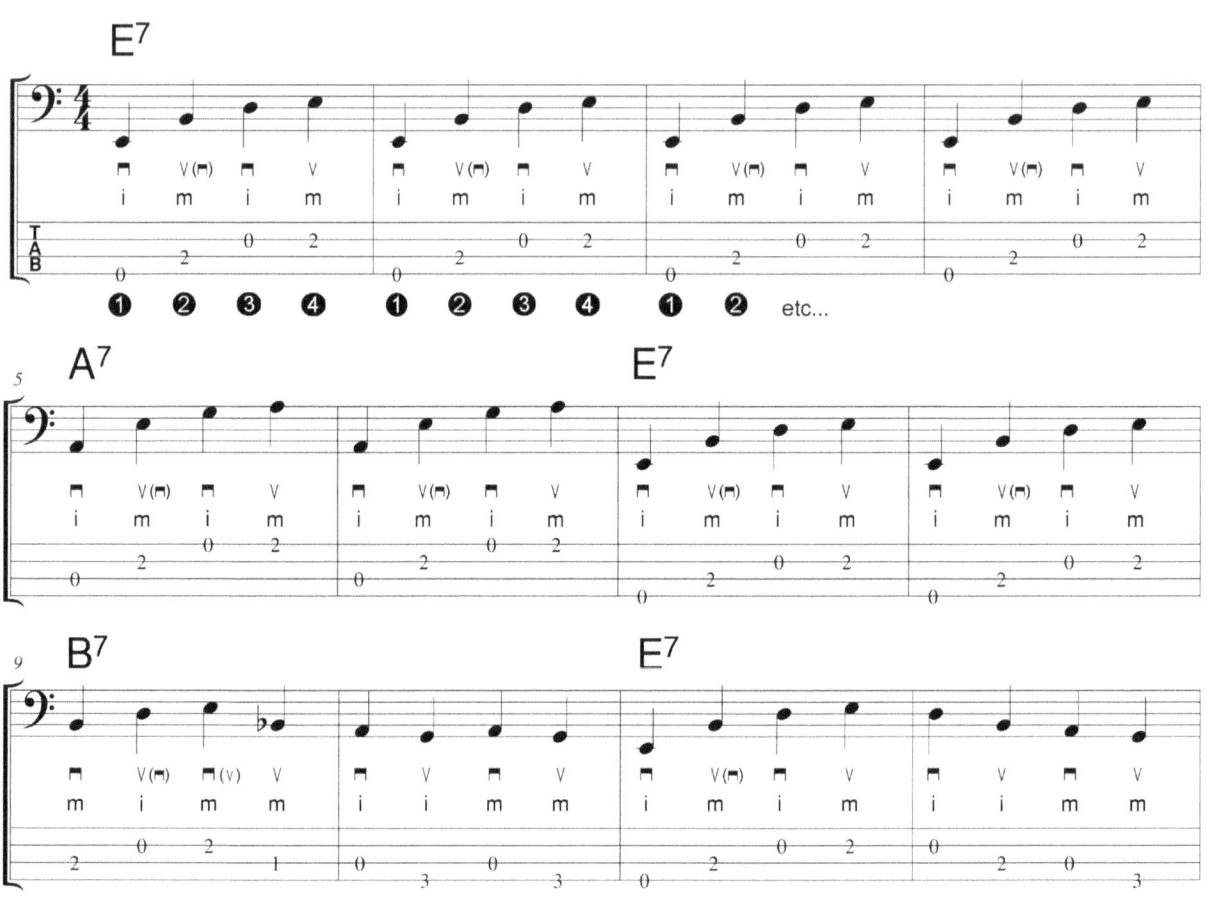

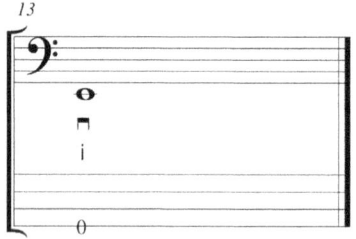

48

Chapter 2 questions

1. *What is the term for a note that could be known as either a sharp (♯) or flat (♭)?*

2. *When going across the same string how many frets apart are the notes A and G?*

3. *When going across the same string how many frets apart are the notes E and F?*

4. *What is an octave?*

5. *What is the sequence of Tones and Semitones for the major scale?*

6. *What note is the 2nd interval of a C major scale?*

7. *What note is the 3rd interval of an E major scale?*

8. *What note is the 6th interval of a D major scale?*

9. *What do arches and downward points represent?*

10. *Name the fundamental shapes for the major scale.*

11. *When moving a shape around the fret-board does the shape change?*

12. *When moving a shape around the fret-board does the root note and therefore scale change?*

13. *What are the intervals of a major triad?*

14. *What are the intervals of a minor triad?*

(You will find the answers at the back of the book)

3 Reading Rhythm

Sight Reading

So far, for the previous musical exercises, numbers have been placed below to help with the rhythm because tablature on its own gives little indication about this. Often when someone wants to learn a favourite song, they get the tablature, and although being familiar with the piece and having a "feel" for it is good, unless we are perfect at that, rhythm reading can help ensure we are playing all of it right. So to get a full idea of a piece the Bassist should at least learn some rhythm reading from the staff.

How long in time a note lasts, is the *note value,* which is indicated by what symbol is used for the note. The following three are commonly used note values…

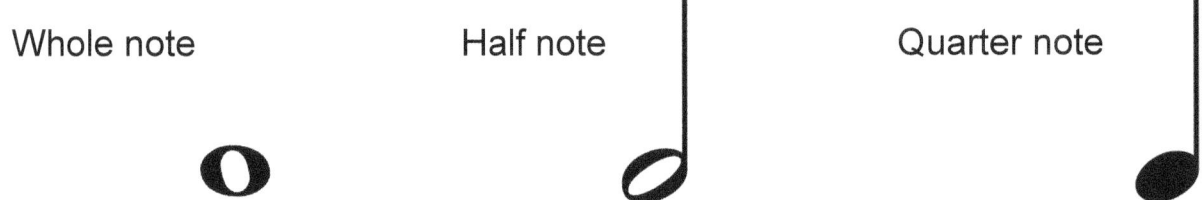

Here are these note values relative to each other…

1 Whole note   =   2 Half notes   =   4 Quarter notes

When you tap your foot or count over a piece of music these are the *beats*. To tell us how to count a piece of music a *Time signature* is used. This appears on the Staff at the start of a piece, just to the right of the clef as two numbers, one on top of the other. The example below shows the Staff as it normally would be above the tab…

The top number tells us how many beats there are in each bar, while the number below tells us what kind of note value the beats are.

When the bottom number is 4 it's quarter notes ♩, so the time signature in the example tells us that there are four quarter note beats per bar. You can count this as *"One Two Three Four"* as shown below…

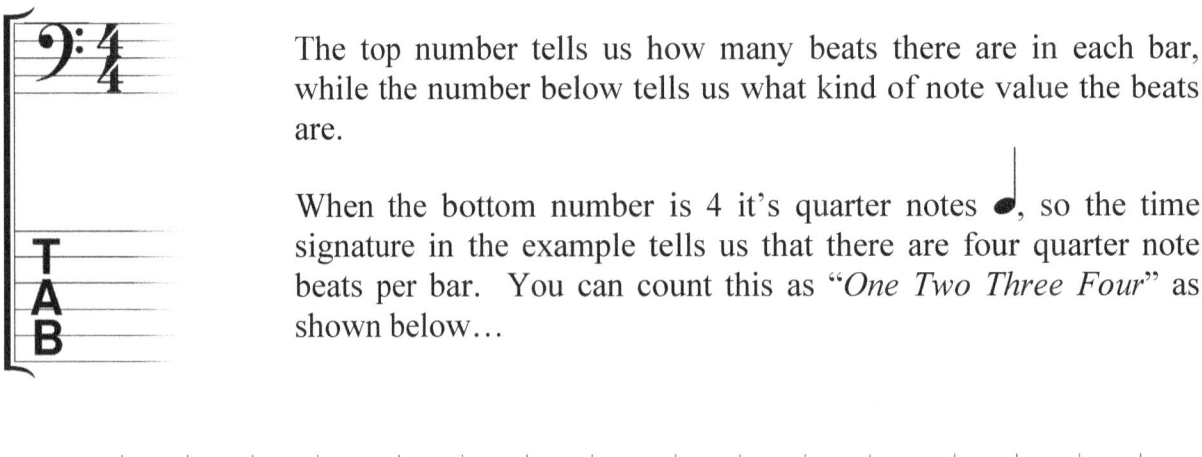

50

You don't have to *play* four quarter notes per bar. There can be any kind of actual notes as long as they add up to fit the duration of the bar, such as in the following example.

Two half notes in the first bar followed by two quarter notes and a half note in the next bar…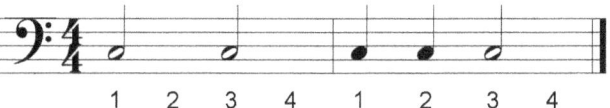

Here are a couple of rhythms for you to try. They are in 4 / 4 time and use the three note values we've just covered. Numbers have been added underneath to help with counting the bars. Clap or play on the Bass (any open string or the note of B for the actual note written) where the notes occur…

1.

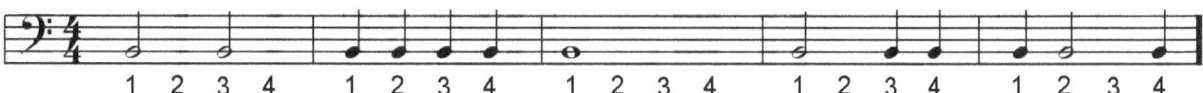

2.

A *Rest* is a pause in music, indicating when *not* to play. Every note value has an equivalent rest. Here are the note values relative to each other again, but with their corresponding rests included underneath…

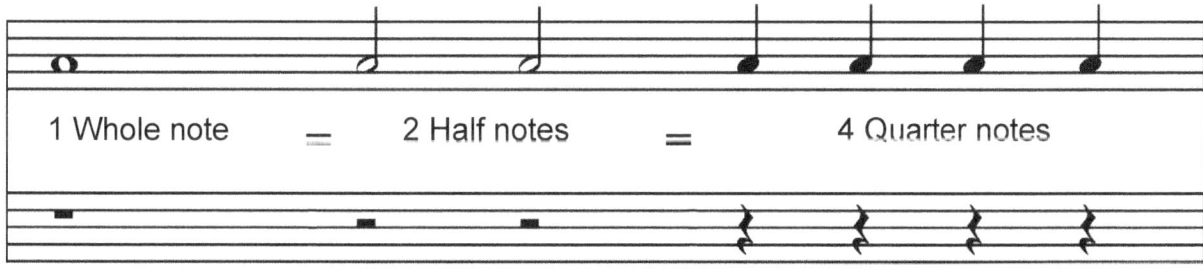

When there is a rest you need to stop the strings from sounding. Use your plucking hand or finger to rest on the string(s) until the next note occurs. This is called *string damping.* Alternatively you could use the fretting hand by gently releasing the pressure from the fretting finger.

Here are a couple of rhythms. Again they are in 4 / 4 time and use the three note values, but now some are rests. It would be better to play them on the Bass rather than clap so that you can account for the rests…

1.

2.

Let's look at another two kinds of smaller note values. The Eighth note and Sixteenth note…

Here are these note values relative to a quarter note and to each other, with their corresponding rests included underneath. When note values smaller than a quarter note occur next to each other, their stems are often barred together.

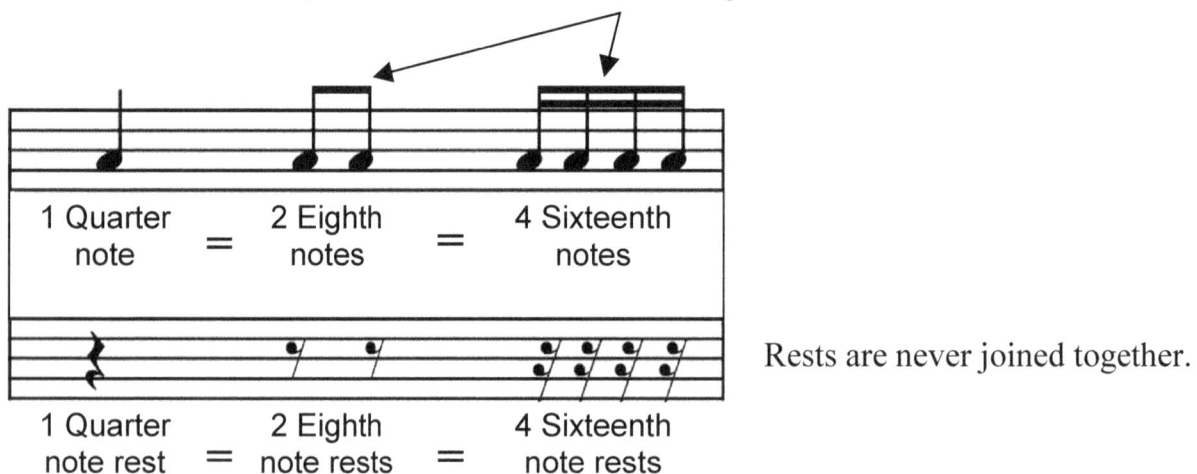

Rests are never joined together.

There are some rhythms that contain these note values on the next section "How to keep time". For now let's look at some more time signatures.

So far we have only looked at 4 / 4 time, the most common time signature, sometimes indicated with a large "C" for "common time". Below are some examples of other types of time signature.

Three quarter note beats per bar…

When the bottom number is 2 this refers to half notes ♩ therefore this time signature is two half note beats per bar…

When the bottom number is 8 this refers to eighth notes ♪ therefore this time signature is six eighth note beats per bar...

What do you think these time signatures mean?

An example of 9/8 time would be the Carpet-baggers theme tune from Jimmy Smith's Album "The Cat". If you listen you might tell its timing is odd. These last two time signatures are known as *odd time*.

How to keep time...when reading rhythm from the staff

To read music rhythm accurately, you need to take into account where in time all the notes are within each bar. To do this we need to count. How to count will depend on what the smallest note value is.

The following explanations show how this is done. The strongest beat(s) are written in **bold** as it helps to emphasise these while counting. Following each explanation is a rhythmical exercise to clap or play while counting.

If any piece is in 4 / 4 time and has no smaller note value than quarter notes, counting "***One** Two Three Four*" or "***One** Two **Three** Four*" is appropriate...

If any piece is in 4 / 4 time and has no smaller note value than eighth notes, counting "***One** and Two and Three and Four and*" or "***One** and Two and **Three** and Four and*" enables us to account for the eighth notes too...

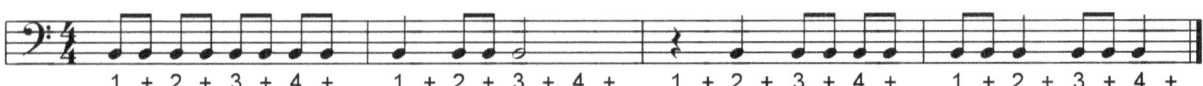

For 3 / 4 time, when quarter notes are the smallest note value you would count "***One** Two Three*"...

In 3 / 4 time, if eighth notes are the smallest note value, counting "***One** and Two and Three and*" enables us to account for the eighth notes too...

If any piece is in 6 / 8 and there is no smaller note value than eighth notes we can count "**One** Two Three **Four** Five Six"…

If in a 4 / 4 piece of music sixteenth notes are the smallest note value we can count "**One** e and a Two e and a Three e and a Four e and a" or "**One** e and a Two e and a **Three** e and a Four e and a" to take the sixteenth notes into account also…

There are other time signatures but these are the most often used. The same principle always applies; count according to the smallest note value and emphasise the strongest beat(s).

Rhythm Exercises

Ex. 1

Tip: Keep time by counting and / or tapping your foot. You can count out loud if it helps.

Ex. 2

Ex. 3

Ex. 4

Ex. 5

Ex. 6

Dotted notes - A dot just after a note increases its value by half.

Half of a half note is a quarter note, so a dotted half note lasts a quarter note longer (or three quarter notes altogether).

Here are some rhythm exercises. They happen to be on the note of D which means the stem of the note goes down to keep it neat (as was explained on the bottom of page 12)…

1.

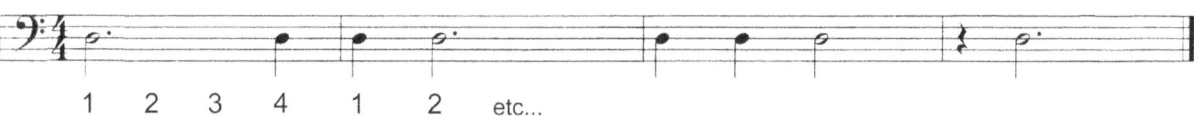

1   2   3   4   1   2   etc…

2.

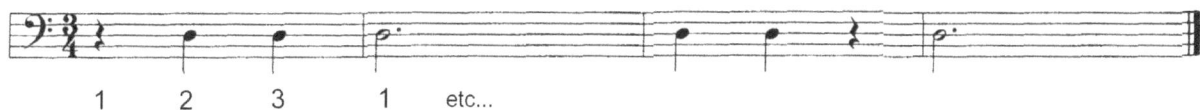

1   2   3   1   etc…

Half of a quarter note is an eighth note, so a dotted quarter note lasts an eighth note longer (or three eighth notes altogether).

Here are some rhythm exercises…

1.

1 + 2 + 3 + 4 +   1 + 2 etc…

2.

1 2 3 4 5 6   1 2 etc…

Tied Notes

A tie is a curved line connecting two notes of the same pitch. When two notes are tied the first note is extended by the value of the note that it is tied to, so the first note lasts longer. Below are a few examples.

Here a half note is tied to an eighth note, making it last an eighth note longer. You could also see this as lasting for two quarter notes and an eighth note (or five eighth notes)….

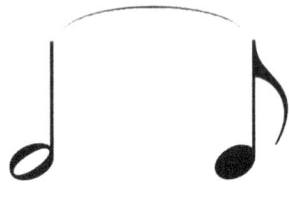

Here an eighth note is tied to a quarter note making it last a quarter note longer. You could also see this as lasting for three eighth notes…

Here a quarter note is tied to a half note. You could also see this as lasting for three quarter notes…

Here are rhythm exercises that have some tied notes. Remember the tied note is held, *not* played as though it's a new note…

1.

2.

Here's one with both dotted notes and tied notes…

Now that we've looked at the rhythmical aspect of conventional notation, for the remainder of the book there will be no more rhythm guide numbers under the pieces so feel free to refer to this section for guidance if need be. The following sample pieces are relatively simple rhythmically. Later on in chapter 6 "Further Techniques" the rhythms become more complex.

Sample Pieces

Here's a simple Rock riff in 4 / 4 time using mostly eighth notes. It may help to emphasise the eighth note on every fourth beat. Don't forget the pause on the 5th bar.

Rock Riff 1 19 & 20

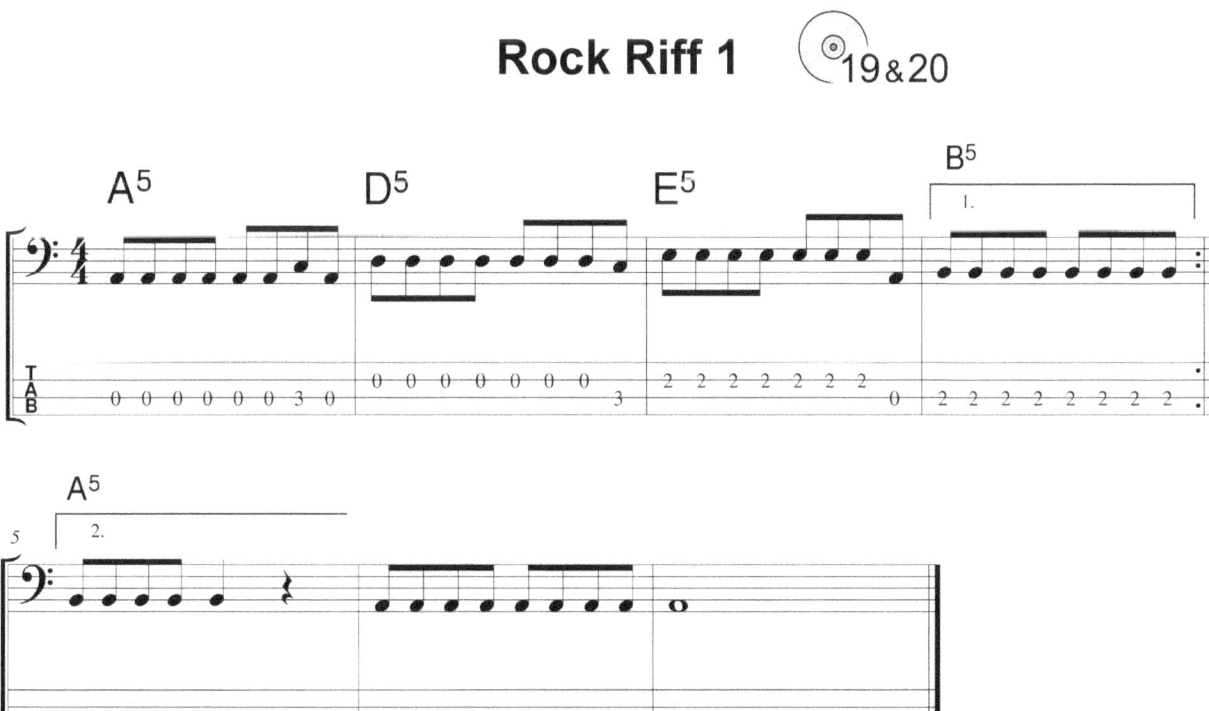

For the following piece rather than trying to follow the actual eighth notes just count "*1 and 2 and 3 and 4 and*" from one bar to the next while playing the eighth notes. Be aware that from the second line the guitar chord (A5) comes in one eighth note earlier just before the next bar so don't let this throw you off the rhythm. There is a temporary break from the eighth note pulse on bar 12.

Rock Riff 2

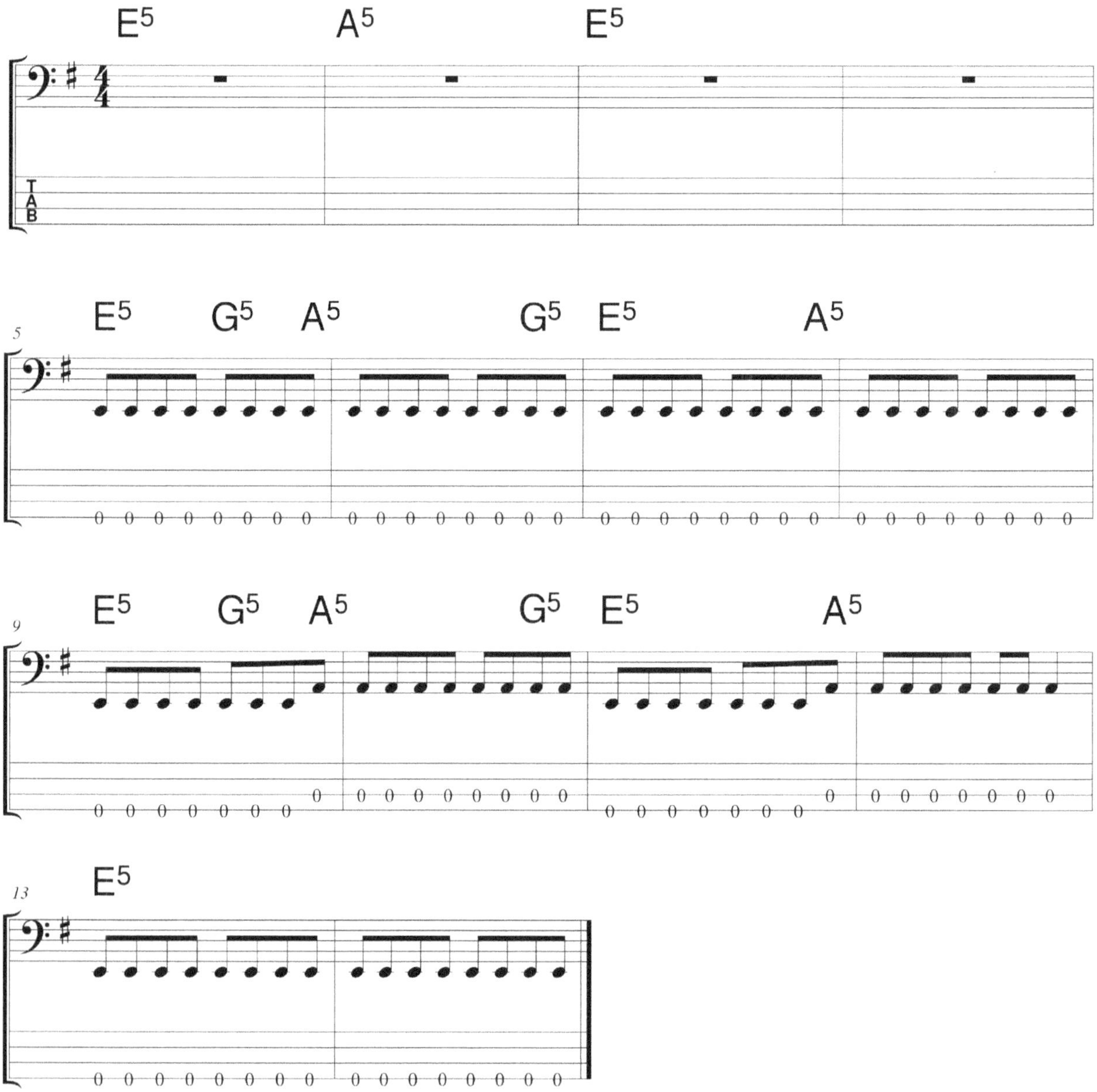

The Bass line for this Cajun style piece is more sparse than the previous two. If you can get the notes in the right place for the 1st bar then most of the rest of the piece has the same rhythm. Bars 6 and 12 are slightly different.

Bayou Noir

This piece is in 6 / 8 time and has "**D.C.**" at the end which stands for *Da capo*, meaning "from the head" in other words go back to the beginning where the whole piece is played again including the repeat. Remember that to help keep time you can emphasise the stronger beats while you count...

Calm Beach

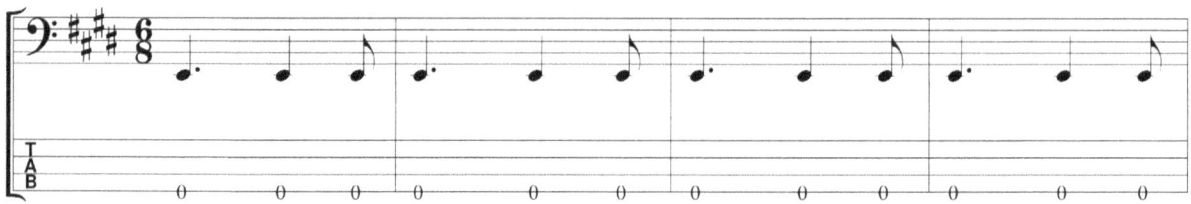

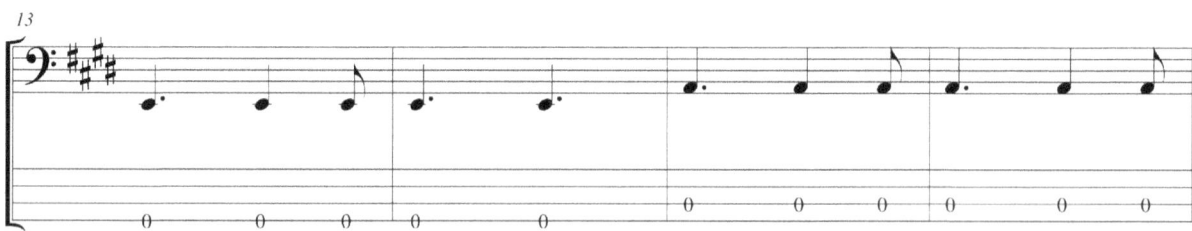

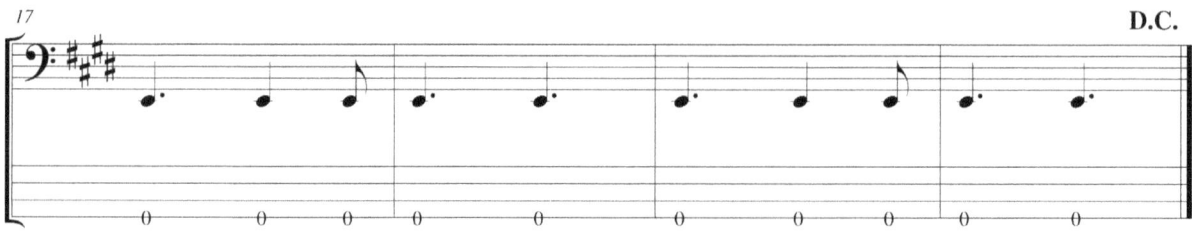

Like the first two Rock riffs, most of the Bass line for this one is an eighth note pulse. The first two repeating introduction bars use a different rhythm. Watch out for the eighth note rest at the start of bar 5.

Rock Riff 3

Chapter 3 questions

1. *What does the "note value" mean?*

2. *How many quarter notes in a whole note?*

3. *How many quarter notes in a half note?*

4. *What does the top number in a time signature tell us?*

5. *What does the bottom number in a time signature tell us?*

6. *What does this time signature mean?*

7. *What kind of note value is this?*

8. *How many of them in a quarter note?*

9. *What kind of rest is this?*

10. *When note values less than a quarter note occur next to each other what often happens to their stems?*

11. *When counting to a piece of music it helps to emphasise what beats?*

12. *How much does a dot just after a note extend the note by?*

13. *If a note lasts longer than the bar that it is in, what can be used to solve this?*

14. *What is the value of this note i.e. how long would it last?* 𝐨.

15. *When two notes are tied together how many notes do you actually play?*

7th Arpeggios

As was originally explained on page 39 chords are made by using odd numbered intervals. So far we have looked at major and minor triads. The next step is to include the interval of the 7th as well, which gives us aptly named 7th chords.

Major 7th

The major 7th chord consists of the **Root, 3rd, 5th and 7th**. Here are the shapes for the major 7th arpeggio...

Low

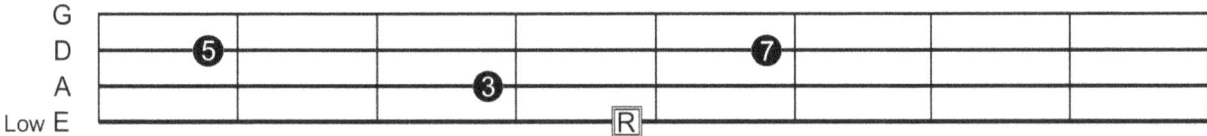

Mid

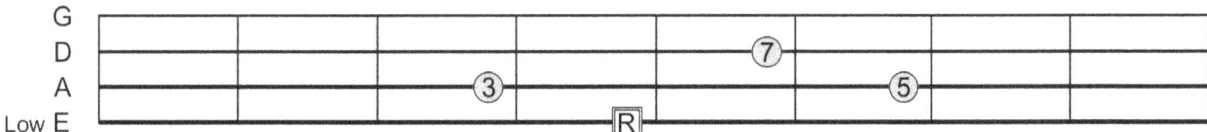

Upper

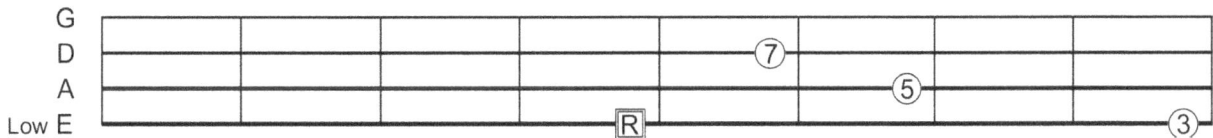

Both the Low and Upper span more frets so the easiest to play will be the Mid.

The piece on the next page uses major 7th arpeggios from the Low and Mid shapes...

> **Note:** The rhythm for the following pieces has been kept simple so we can get used to the arpeggios, although if you feel confident you could make up your own Bass lines with them.

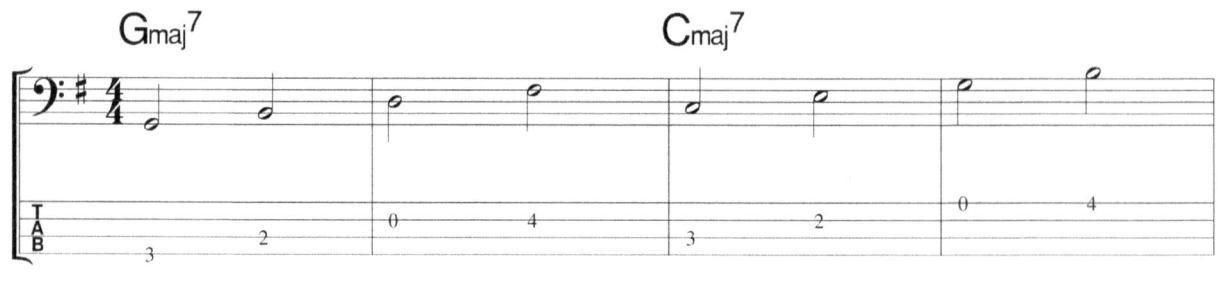

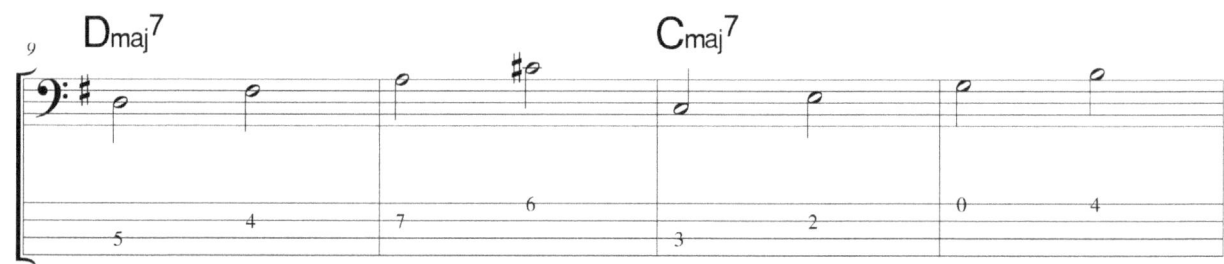
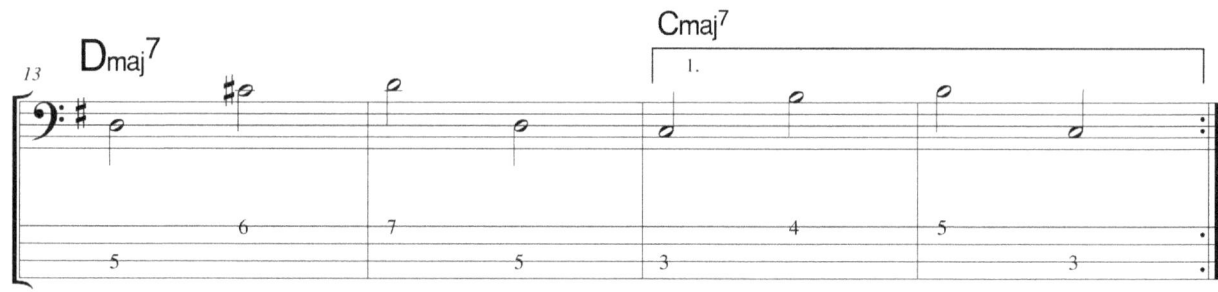
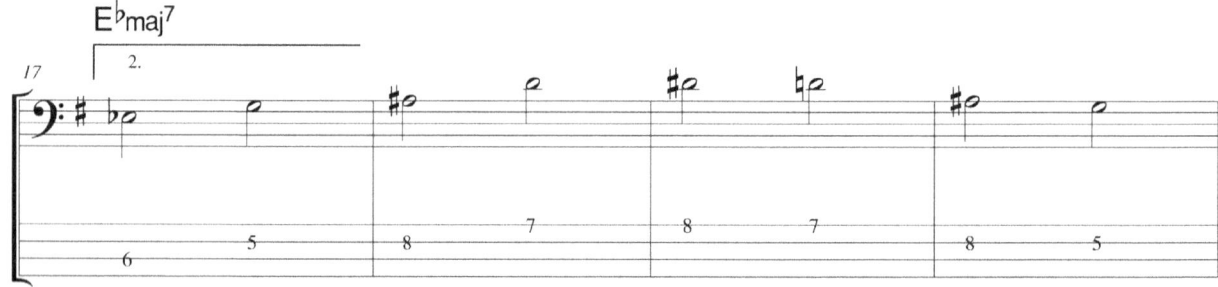
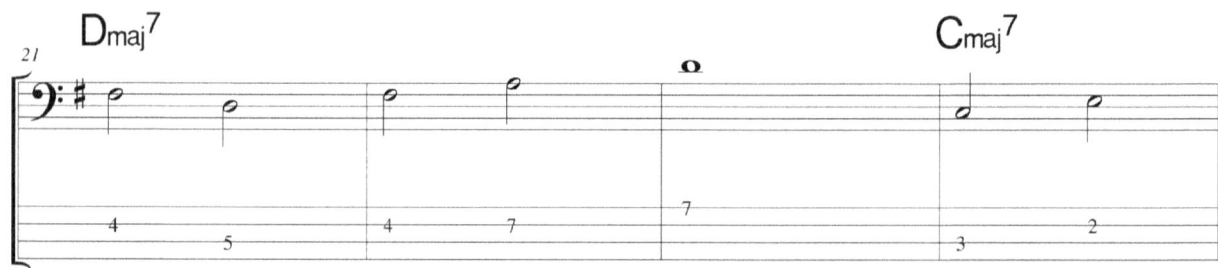

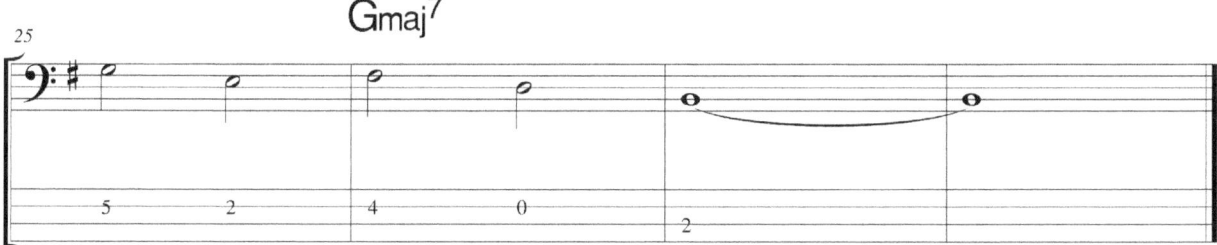

Minor 7th

The minor 7th chord consists of the intervals **Root, minor 3rd, 5th and minor 7th**. Here are the shapes for the minor 7th arpeggio…

Low

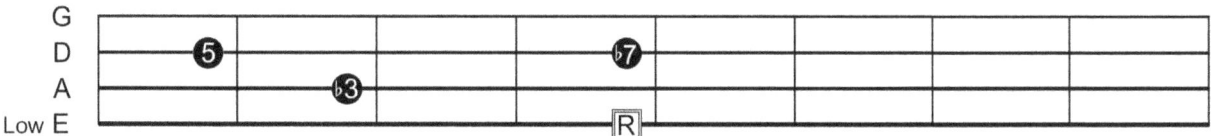

Mid

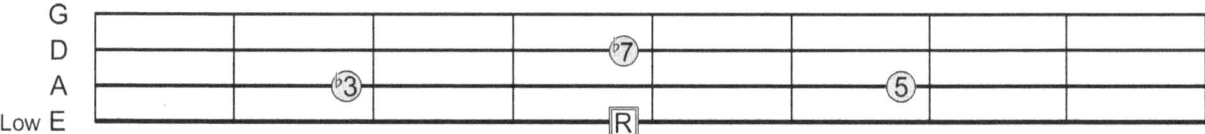

Upper

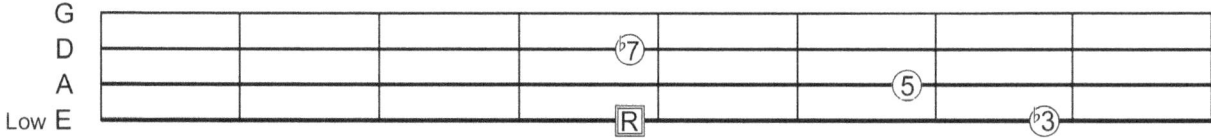

Mid spans more frets, Low and Upper will be the easiest to play.

For the following piece over the page, on bar 18 is "**D.C. al Coda**". D.C. as mentioned earlier (on page 64) stands for *Da Capo* meaning from the head (go back to the beginning). Al coda stands for *apply the coda*. The coda acts like a teleport.

The playing directions are as follows: Play from the start to bar 8 then repeat, but this time skip from bar 6 to bar 9. Continue to bar 18 (where you see **D.C. al Coda**) then go back to the start of the piece. The coda at the end of bar 6 takes you to bar 19 from where you continue to the end of the piece. The piece uses minor 7th arpeggios from the Low, Mid and Upper shapes...

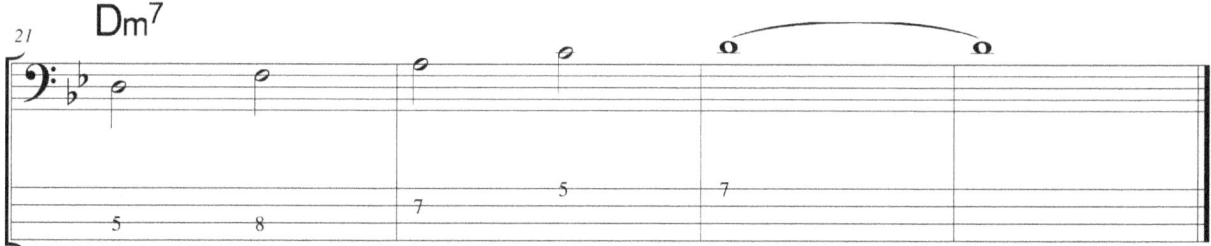

Dominant 7th

The Dominant 7th chord consists of the **Root, 3rd, 5th and minor 7th**. Here are the arpeggios…

Low

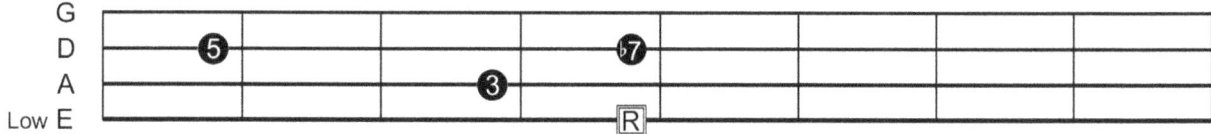

Mid

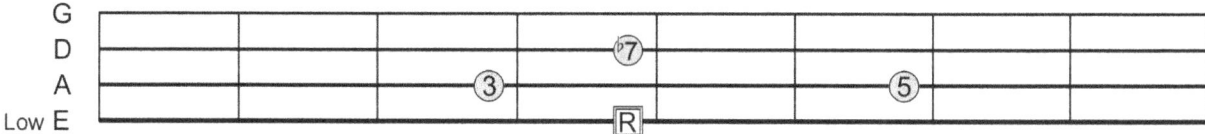

Upper

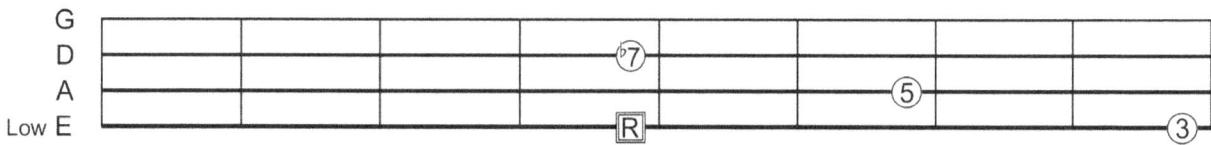

The easiest of the three are the Low and Mid as they span less frets.

The following piece uses Dominant 7th arpeggios from all three shapes. The Upper is used for when the root note is on an open string…

Here's a piece that uses major 7th, minor 7th and Dominant 7th arpeggios. On bar 17 there is a minor7♭5 chord (this type of chord will be covered later)…

7th Arpeggios

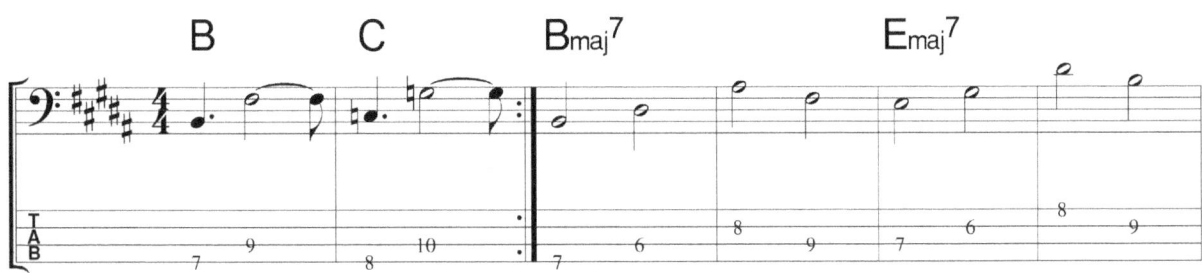

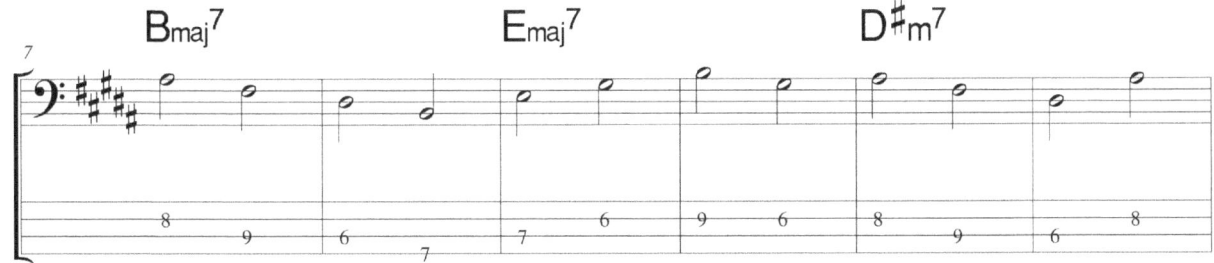

Here's another piece that uses all three types of 7th arpeggio covered so far…

7th Arpeggios (2)

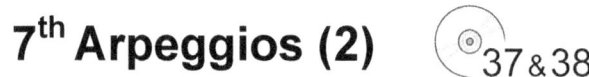

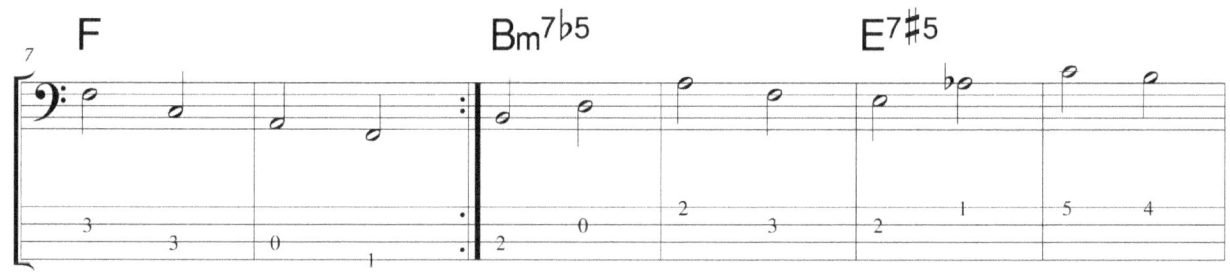

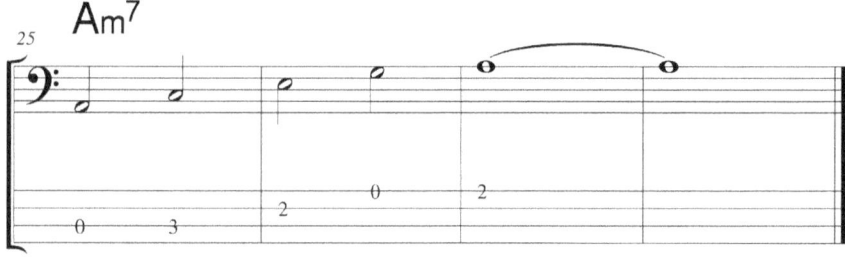

Chapter 4 questions

1. *What are the intervals of a Major 7th arpeggio?*

2. *What are the intervals of a Minor 7th arpeggio?*

3. *What are the intervals of a Dominant 7th arpeggio?*

4. *What shape for the Major 7th arpeggio spans the least frets?*

5. *What shape for the Dominant 7th arpeggio spans the most frets?*

6. *What does "**D.C.**" mean?*

7. *What is this?:*

5 Modes and Harmony

Modes of the Major Scale

The next part of the book (up to page 92) gets tougher and is best absorbed over a period of time so don't expect to understand all of it immediately and don't wait until you do before moving onto anything else. As we now know Bass lines are often based around notes from within chords, therefore it is fairly important for a bassist to understand the subjects covered in this section.

Back to the all-important major scale. If we start and finish the major scale on a note other than its root then we have shifted the tonal centre, giving us a new kind of scale called a *mode*, of which there are seven (seeing as the major scale is made of seven notes). All of the modes will contain only the notes of the major scale that they come from, in this context the major scale is known as the *Parent scale*.

In order to do this we will need the Parent major scale to go through more than one octave. The linear layout of piano keys can be used to demonstrate this more simply.

In the diagram below, D major scale is shown repeating through two octaves. In order to start and finish from the 2nd interval (the note of E), we need to start on the 2nd within one octave of the Parent major scale then finish on the 2nd within the next octave. In the diagram this has been demonstrated, as well as for the 3rd interval from F♯ to F♯…

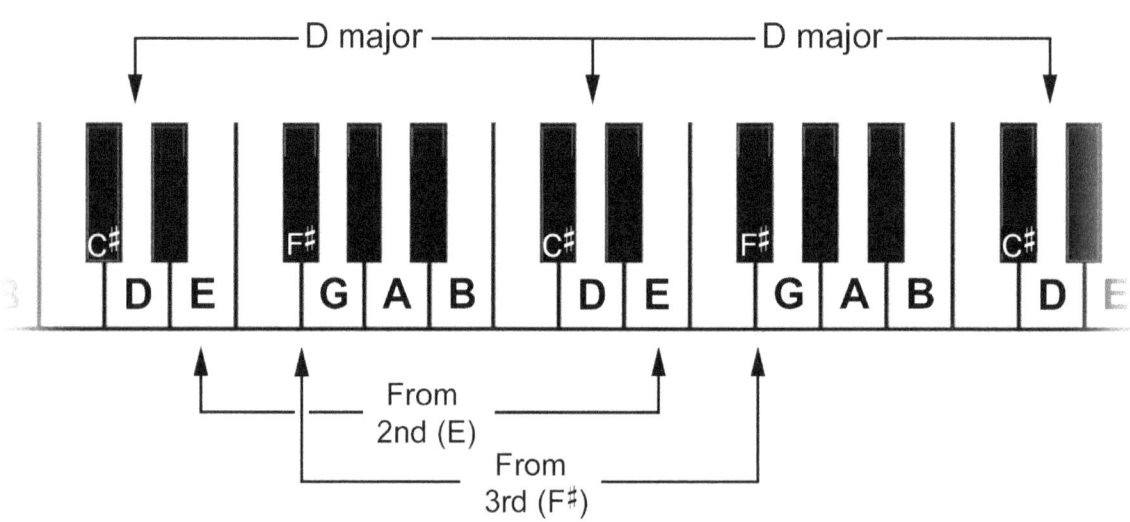

It wouldn't be possible to do this within one octave of the Parent scale because obviously you would be limited to only one place for each interval.

To play the major scale through more than one octave on the fret-board we can alternate between fundamental shapes to keep the hand in the same area. Below is the Mid shape with its root on the low E string, having been continued through another higher octave using the Low shape…

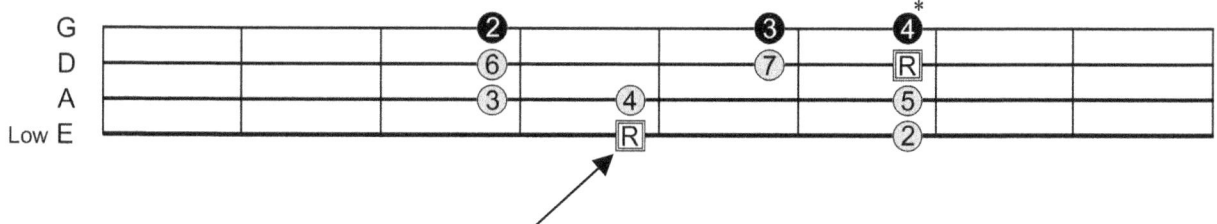

The starting root note on the low E string and therefore the scale, is shown on no particular fret because the scale shape will be the same whichever fret it starts on, so you can choose where to start. On the 10th fret would be a D major scale similar to the one used for the piano example on the previous page.

Note: * The Low shape ends on the interval of the 4th, that's as far as the strings take us without moving up the fret-board. Had we continued through the next octave by using the same mid shape the hand would have to shift further up the fret-board. There's nothing wrong with that approach, but combining the different fundamental shapes this way makes it easier to manoeuvre the hand within the same area and is basically the same principle behind the C A G E D system for the six-string guitar.

Let's start on the 2nd interval to shift the tonal centre. Here it starts and ends on the 2nd interval which we can now regard as a new root note…

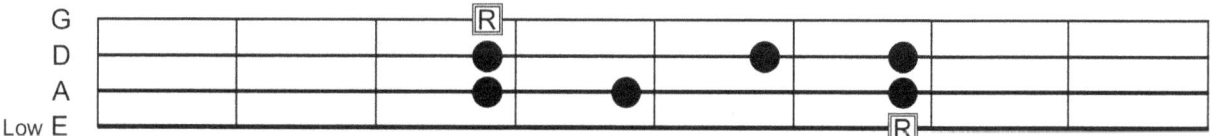

To define the modes, rather than saying "The major scale started from its 2nd interval" or "The major scale started from its 5th interval" etc we need to see the mode as a new scale, then if we compare it to the shape of the major scale started from the same root we can see what the intervals are. The major scale shape we are comparing the new mode to is only for this purpose and NOT part of the process of modes from the major scale.

To find out which of the three fundamental major scale shapes to compare to, the clue is in how many notes are on the string that the root note is on, including the root note itself (this method of identification was originally mentioned on page 35). In this case there is one, the root note itself, so the shape looks closest to the *Low* (which is why it has been shade coded black) therefore we need to compare it to that.

When comparing our new mode to the major scale Low shape we can see that the 3rd and the 7th are not in the same place, they are a semitone lower. Here's the comparison…

Major Scale Low shape

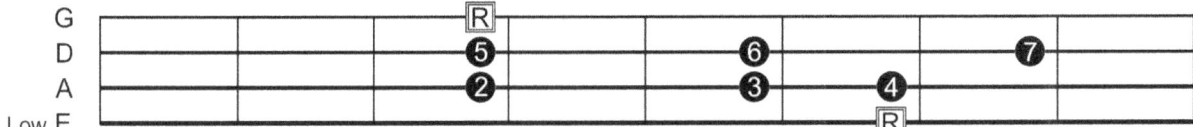

Compared to New Mode

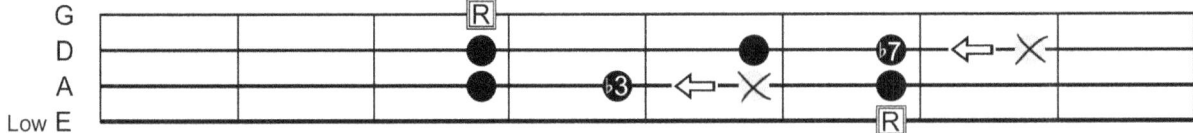

New mode (with intervals that are different indicated)

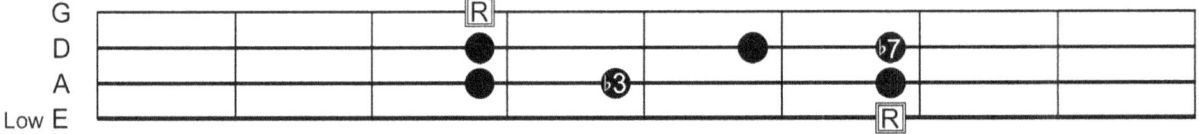

So the intervals are 1 2 ♭3 4 5 6 ♭7 This is the **Dorian** mode. Here's the Dorian mode shown in intervals having been taken from the Parent major scale…

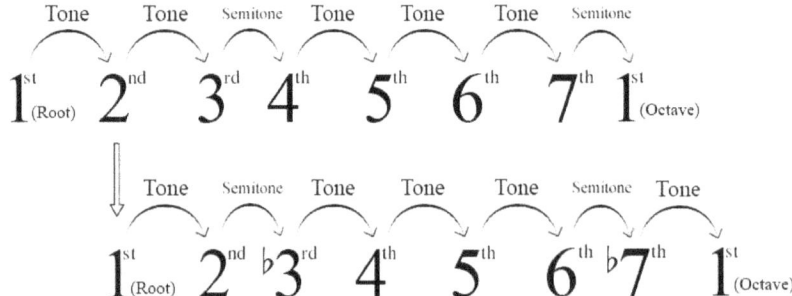

Phrygian

On to the next mode. On the next page is the parent major scale started from its 3rd interval. It has three notes on the string that the root note is on, so looks closest to, and has therefore been compared to the Upper major scale shape. The intervals that are different have been indicated…

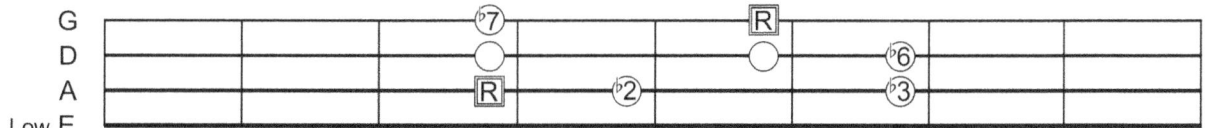

The intervals for this mode are 1 ♭2 ♭3 4 5 ♭6 ♭7   Here's the Phrygian mode taken from the Parent major scale shown in intervals…

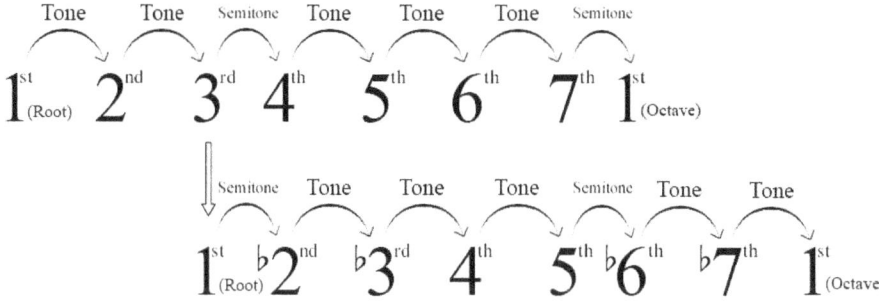

Lydian

The Parent major scale started from its 4th interval. It has two notes on the string that the root note is on, so looks closest to, and has therefore been compared to the Mid major scale shape. The interval that is different has been indicated…

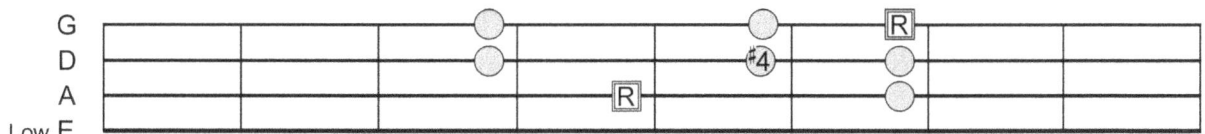

The intervals for this mode are 1 2 3 ♯4 5 6 7   Here's the Lydian mode from the Parent major scale shown in intervals…

By now you should have an idea of how modes work as "scales within a scale". So far, taking them from within the Parent major scale shape on page 77 has shown graphically on the fret-board how the modes can be found. However in order to continue through the next three modes we would need to go further up the G string outside the shape. On an instrument with more strings (such as the 6 string guitar or a 5 string Bass) this wouldn't be the case. This is by no means a limitation of the four string Bass in general it's just that it has four strings.

Mixolydian

Here's the Parent major scale started from its 5th interval. For this mode the higher octave of the root note goes outside the Parent major scale shape by two frets. It looks closest to, and has therefore been compared to the Low major scale shape. The interval that is different has been indicated...

The intervals for this mode are 1 2 3 4 5 6 ♭7   Here's the Mixolydian mode from the Parent major scale shown in intervals...

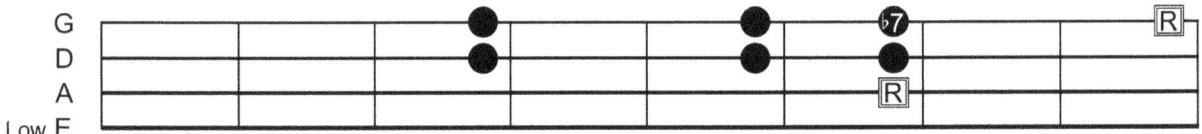

Aeolian (Natural minor)

For the next mode based on the 6th interval, rather than continuing upward we're going to go *behind* the Parent major scale shape. This is the same principle as extending the Parent major scale through more than one octave (as originally explained on pages 76 - 77) except now we are extending it *downward* rather than upward.

According to the TTSTTTS formula for the major scale, if we go backwards from the root, the 6th can be found a semitone and a tone (three frets) below...

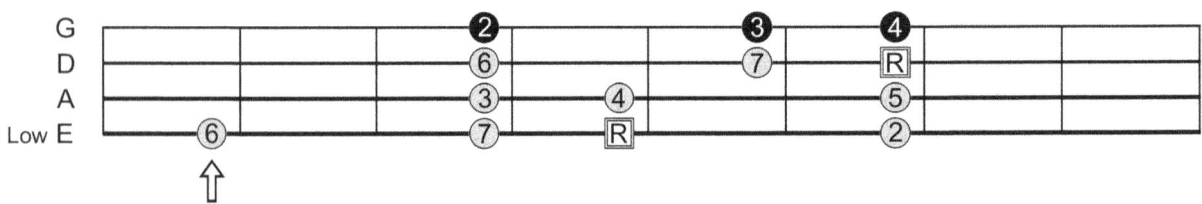

80

Here is the Aeolian. It has three notes on the string that the root note is on so looks closest to, and has therefore been compared to, the Upper major scale shape. The intervals that are different have been indicated...

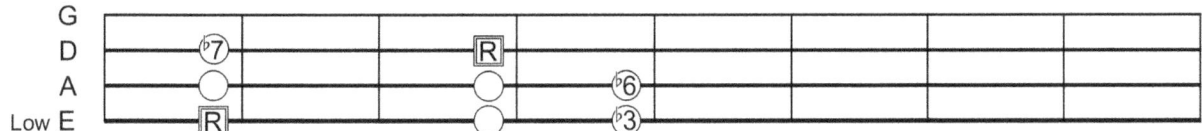

The intervals for this mode are 1 2 b3 4 5 b6 b7 Here's the Aeolian mode from the Parent major scale shown in intervals...

Locrian

The mode based on the 7th interval has been found in a similar way to the Aeolian by going behind the shape for the major Parent scale. This time it's a semitone (one fret) behind. Most of the intervals for this one are from within the original shape for the Parent major scale, the only one that isn't is its lower root note. It looks closest to, and has therefore has been compared to, the Upper major scale shape. The intervals that are different have been indicated...

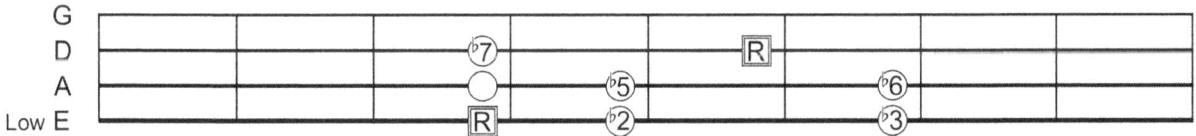

The intervals for this mode are 1 b2 b3 4 b5 b6 b7 Here's the Locrian mode from the Parent major scale shown in intervals...

The modal name for the major scale itself is *Ionian* (the names for the modes come from ancient Greek civilisations). Here are all the modes and their intervals…

Ionian (Major)	1	2	3	4	5	6	7
Dorian	1	2	♭3	4	5	6	♭7
Phrygian	1	♭2	♭3	4	5	♭6	♭7
Lydian	1	2	3	♯4	5	6	7
Mixolydian	1	2	3	4	5	6	♭7
Aeolian (Natural minor)	1	2	♭3	4	5	♭6	♭7
Locrian	1	♭2	♭3	4	♭5	♭6	♭7

As previously mentioned on page 30 when music is referred to as being in a certain *Key* (such as D major, E♭ major or A major etc), this means it is based on that scale. So music in the key of D major would be based on the D major scale and something in the key of E♭ major based on the E♭ major scale. Whatever major scale you used for the modes would be the key so had you chosen D major you would have been in the key of D major. Eventually this will show us what we can do with the major scale and the basics of how chords are arranged.

There are also minor keys based on the minor scale, covered on the next page…

Modes of the Minor Scale

So far we have dealt with the major scale, the 6th mode of which (Aeolian) is also known as the *Natural minor* scale. This scale can be regarded as its own key centre to give us *minor keys* (as opposed to music in major keys based on the major scale). These scales are known as *relative* and every major scale / key has a relative minor scale / key. The modes of the natural minor scale will be the same as the ones for the major scale starting from the 6th (Aeolian)…

Mode		Intervals
Aeolian (Natural minor)		*1 2 b3 4 5 b6 b7
Locrian		1 b2 b3 4 b5 b6 b7
Ionian (Major)		1 2 3 4 5 6 7
Dorian		1 2 b3 4 5 6 b7
Phrygian		1 b2 b3 4 5 b6 b7
Lydian		1 2 3 #4 5 6 7
Mixolydian		1 2 3 4 5 6 b7

* Remember that in a minor key the modes will now start on intervals from the Parent *minor* scale, which are **Root, 2nd, minor 3rd, 4th, 5th, minor 6th and minor 7th**

The **Aeolian** mode is the parent minor scale on the **1st** (root)

The **Locrian** mode   will be on the   **2nd**   of the parent minor scale.

The **Ionian** mode   will be on the   **minor 3rd**   of the parent minor scale.

The **Dorian** mode   will be on the   **4th**   of the parent minor scale.

The **Phrygian** mode   will be on the   **5th**   of the parent minor scale.

The **Lydian** mode   will be on the   **minor 6th**   of the parent minor scale.

The **Mixolydian** mode   will be on the   **minor 7th**   of the parent minor scale.

Harmonising

Now for the chords / arpeggios. Earlier (page 39) it was explained how chords are made at the first and most basic level, by using odd numbered intervals from a scale. For instance the Root, 3rd and 5th taken from the major scale give us a major triad based chord. We can also get chords from the modes by taking the odd numbered intervals from them. This is known as *harmonising*. In the following diagram these intervals are circled for each mode. To the right of that the intervals are shown together (Triad), and to the very right the chord type that it is. The dotted box around Ionian and Aeolian indicate key centres for relative major and minor…

Mode	Intervals	Triad	Chord
Ionian (Major)	①　2　③　4　⑤　6　7	1　3　5	Major
Dorian	①　2　♭③　4　⑤　6　♭7	1　♭3　5	minor
Phrygian	①　♭2　♭③　4　⑤　♭6　♭7	1　♭3　5	minor
Lydian	①　2　③　♯4　⑤　6　7	1　3　5	Major
Mixolydian	①　2　③　4　⑤　6　♭7	1　3　5	Major
Aeolian (Natural minor)	①　2　♭③　4　⑤　♭6　♭7	1　♭3　5	minor
Locrian	①　♭2　♭③　4　♭⑤　♭6　♭7	1　♭3　♭5	diminished

The sequence of triad-based chords that we get from the harmonised major scale is…

Major, minor, minor, Major, Major, minor, diminished

The sequence of triad-based chords that we get from the harmonised minor scale is…

minor, diminished, Major, minor, minor, Major, Major

Let's look at how this works on the fret-board. Here are triad arpeggios from harmonised C major. All of these arpeggio shapes come from within the Mid / Low parent major scale shape on page 77 (and therefore each arpeggio shape from its subsequent mode)…

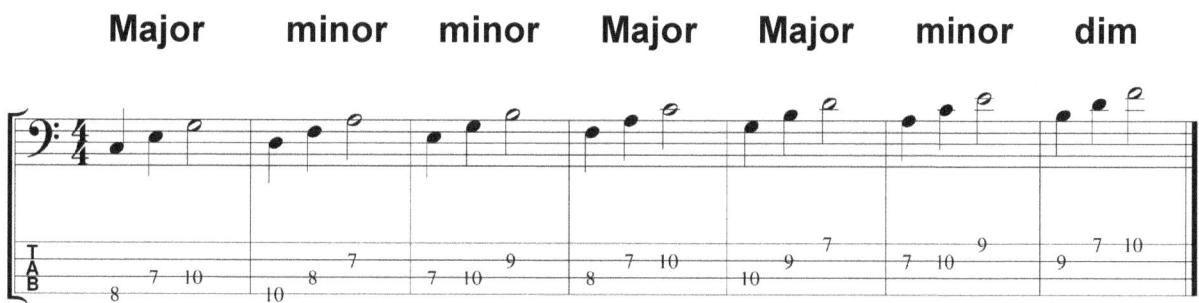

Here they are again but going up one string (A string). This is like the major scale played across one string (like on page 28) but now with an arpeggio from each interval…

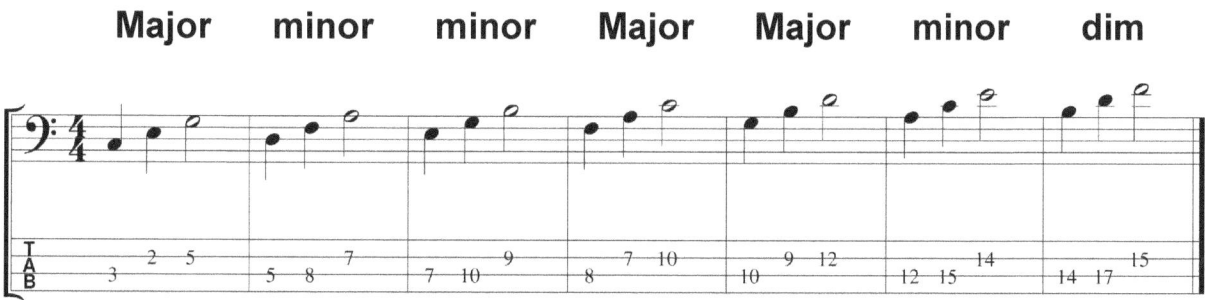

Here are triad arpeggios for A minor (the relative minor of C Major). The shapes for these start from within the shape we made for the Aeolian mode on pages 80 - 81…

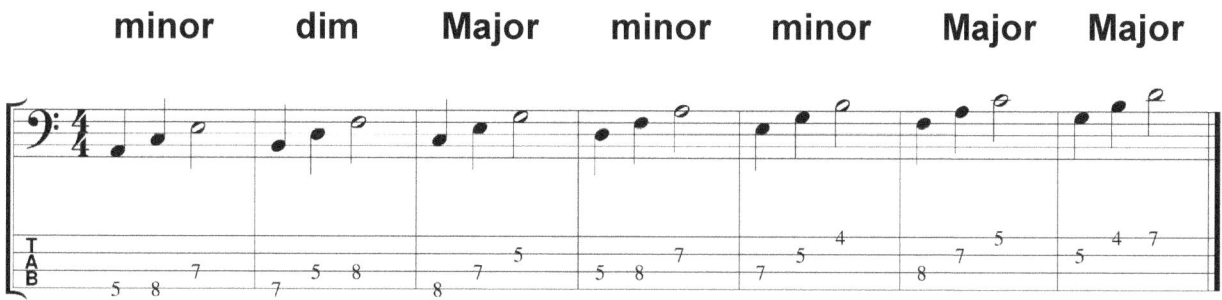

This process can be applied to *any* key. On the next page is a chart in which the process is shown for all the keys. If you write songs it could help as a reference for the arpeggios / chords.

Across the top are the generic intervals and their corresponding modes, across the bottom are the chord types for each. For example the 3rd interval of A major is C♯ from which the mode of Phrygian comes with which a C♯ minor chord would fit…

Major key	1st	2nd	3rd	4th	5th	6th	7th
	Major	Dorian	Phrygian	Lydian	Mixolydian	Aeolian	Locrian
C major	C	D	E	F	G	A	B
G major	G	A	B	C	D	E	F♯
D major	D	E	F♯	G	A	B	C♯
A major	A	B	C♯	D	E	F♯	G♯
E major	E	F♯	G♯	A	B	C♯	D♯
B major	B	C♯	D♯	E	F♯	G♯	A♯
F♯ major	F♯	G♯	A♯	B	C♯	D♯	E♯
C♯ major	C♯	D♯	E♯	F♯	G♯	A♯	B♯
F major	F	G	A	B♭	C	D	E
B♭ major	B♭	C	D	E♭	F	G	A
E♭ major	E♭	F	G	A♭	B♭	C	D
A♭ major	A♭	B♭	C	D♭	E♭	F	G
D♭ major	D♭	E♭	F	G♭	A♭	B♭	C
G♭ major	G♭	A♭	B♭	C♭	D♭	E♭	F
C♭ major	C♭	D♭	E♭	F♭	G♭	A♭	B♭
To 3rd interval of mode →	Major	minor	minor	Major	Major	minor	dim
* To 7th interval of mode →	Maj7	min7	min7	Maj7	Dom7	min7	min7^b5

Dom = Dominant

* Included along the bottom of the chart are the chord types obtained from using the 7th interval of each mode also. There is a further explanation of this process on the following page.

This is simply extending triads by another interval, so now we have chords made from the root, 3rd 5th *and* 7th of each mode (just like "Chapter 4, 7th chords" but now we see how they fit within the key). Here is the same chart from page 84 but now with 7th chords. For the 7th mode (Locrian) we can see the corresponding chord is the minor7♭5 (we came across this chord / arpeggio in the piece on page 73)…

Mode	Intervals	Chord intervals	Chord
Ionian (Major)	① 2 ③ 4 ⑤ 6 ⑦	1 3 5 7	Major7th
Dorian	① 2 ♭③ 4 ⑤ 6 ♭⑦	1 ♭3 5 ♭7	minor7th
Phrygian	① ♭2 ♭③ 4 ⑤ ♭6 ♭⑦	1 ♭3 5 ♭7	minor7th
Lydian	① 2 ③ ♯4 ⑤ 6 ⑦	1 3 5 7	Major7th
Mixolydian	① 2 ③ 4 ⑤ 6 ♭⑦	1 3 5 ♭7	Dom7th
Aeolian (Natural minor)	① 2 ♭③ 4 ⑤ ♭6 ♭⑦	1 ♭3 5 ♭7	minor7th
Locrian	① ♭2 ♭③ 4 ♭⑤ ♭6 ♭⑦	1 ♭3 ♭5 ♭7	minor7♭5

The sequence of 7th chords that we get from the harmonised major scale is…

Major 7th, minor 7th, minor 7th, Major 7th, Dominant 7th, minor 7th, minor 7♭5

The sequence of 7th chords that we get from the harmonised minor scale is…

minor 7th, minor 7♭5, Major 7th, minor 7th, minor 7th, Major 7th, Dominant 7th

Here are 7th arpeggios from harmonised C Major. Again, just like the triad based arpeggios on page 85; all of these arpeggio shapes come from within the Mid / Low parent major scale shape on page 77 (and therefore each arpeggio shape from its subsequent mode)…

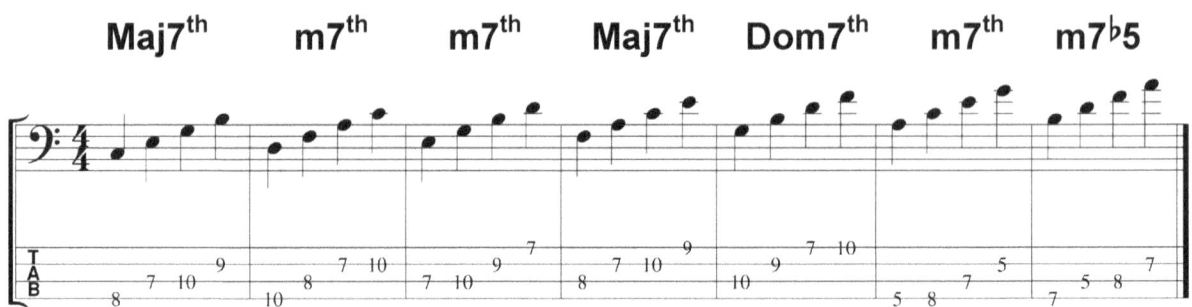

Here they are again going up one string…

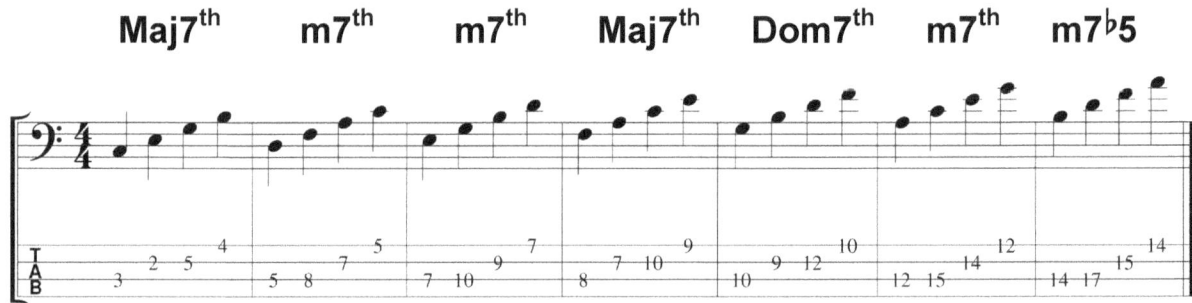

Here are 7th arpeggios for A minor, which is the relative minor of C Major (you could check this on the chart from page 86). Like the previous triad based arpeggios the shapes for these start from within the shape we made for the Aeolian mode on pages 80 - 81…

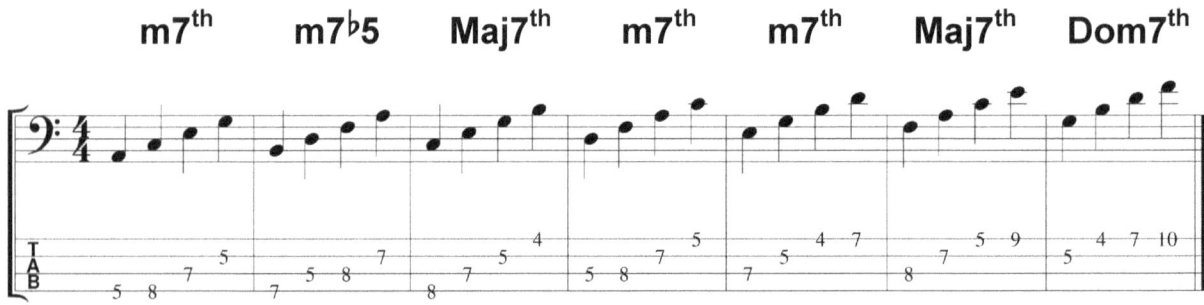

Roman Numerals

The harmonised chord types are the same whatever the key, but rather than describe a chord as for example "The chord from the 4th interval in the key of D major" Roman numerals can be used. (In this section the term "chord" is used but of course it applies to arpeggios too).

Major Keys

Upper and lower case represent the chord type, upper case for major and lower case for minor. The numeric value represents the interval of the parent major scale that the chord comes from (which is the root note of the chord). Here are Roman numerals with the harmonised chords they represent written underneath…

I	ii	iii	IV	V	vi	viio
Major	minor	minor	Major	Major	minor	diminished

With this we can translate a chord sequence into any key. Let's say we have the following chord sequence in the key of A Major, and want to change it to the key of E♭ major…

	C♯m	E	Bm	D	A
In roman numerals that would be…	iii	V	ii	IV	I
In the key of E♭ major…	Gm	B♭	Fm	A♭	E♭

> **Note:** The chart from page 86 can be used to help with the following questions in this tutorial. The answers can be found at the back of the book.

Work out the chord sequence   ii   V   I   IV   in the following keys…

1) D major: _____ _____ _____ _____

2) B♭ major: _____ _____ _____ _____

3) D♭ major: _____   _____   _____   _____

Here are Roman numerals with the 7th chords they represent written underneath…

Imaj⁷	ii⁷	iii⁷	IVmaj⁷	V⁷	vi⁷	vii⁷♭5
Major⁷	minor⁷	minor⁷	Major⁷	Dom⁷	minor⁷	minor⁷♭5

Work out the chord sequence   Imaj⁷   IVmaj⁷   vii⁷♭5   vi⁷   in the following keys…

4) C major: _____   _____   _____   _____

5) A major: _____   _____   _____   _____

6) F major: _____   _____   _____   _____

Triad based chords and 7th chords don't have to be separate, they can and often do exist in the same chord progression. Work out the chord sequence   iii⁷   vi   ii   V⁷   in the following keys…

7) E♭ major: _____   _____   _____   _____

8) B major: _____   _____   _____   _____

9) G major: _____   _____   _____   _____

Minor Keys

For the harmonised natural minor the roman numeric values for the 3rd, 6th and 7th are "flattened" to reflect the intervals of the scale. Here are the roman numerals with what they represent written underneath each…

i	iio	bIII	iv	v	bVI	bVII
minor	diminished	Major	minor	minor	Major	Major

For 7th chords…

i7	ii7b5	bIIImaj7	iv7	v7	bVImaj7	bVII7
minor7	minor7b5	Major7	minor7	minor7	Major7	Dom7

Work out this chord sequence   iv   bIIImaj7   bVII7   i7   in the keys of….

10) C# minor: F#m   Emaj7   B7   C#m7

11) D minor: Gm   Fmaj7   C7   Dm7

12) B minor: Em   Dmaj7   A7   Bm7

In minor keys the minor or min7th chord based on the 5th (v or v7) is often converted to a Major or Dominant 7th chord (V or V7). This is because the minor or min7th chord based on the 5th doesn't have as strong a resolution to the root note of the parent minor scale (also known as the *tonic*). A Major or Dominant 7th chord on the 5th does however, because in relation to the tonic, the interval of the 3rd within these chords is the major 7th which has a stronger resolution to the tonic. The 7th in this context is known as the *leading tone*.

Let's say we are in the key of A minor. Play E minor or Em7 (v or v7) then follow with A minor or Am7 (i or i7). Try again but this time starting with E major or E7 (V or V7). Both sound good but the latter resolves more strongly to the A minor or Am7 chord. Of course this applies to arpeggios too as they are simply chords with their notes played separately.

Work out this chord sequence   ii7b5   bVI   V7   i   in the keys of…

13) E minor: _____ _____ _____ _____

14) B minor: _____ _____ _____ _____

15) C minor: _____ _____ _____ _____

We can see how some of the pieces in the book have been written. For example the piece on page 41, in the key of C major is…

    I   iii   I   iii   IV   V   I   ii   **(repeat)**   I

The Bossa style piece on page 43 in the key of C major is….

    I   IV   ii   vi   IV   iii   **(x3)**   I

Bayou Noir on page 63 in the key of D major is….

    I   V   I   V   etc…

The minor arpeggio piece on page 45 in the key of A minor is…

i   iv   i   iv   v   iv   v   i   (Changes key to C minor)   i   v
i   (Changes key back to A minor)   iv   v   i

Well that's the end of the tough bit. Chord harmony in major or minor keys doesn't cover all aspects of music structure (I'm afraid to say!) it is however the main foundation. Some other potential areas to look at once the concept of modes and chord harmony is grasped include; Modulation (Key Changes in other words), Chord substitution, Modal interchange and Secondary Dominants. When pieces in this book other than the four mentioned above *don't* fit with chord harmony, then one of those will be occurring.

Chapter 5 questions

1. *What is the term used for a scale you get when playing the Major or minor scale from a note other than its root?*

2. *What can we call the Major or minor scale they come from?*

3. *What is the name of the mode from the 2nd interval of the Major scale?*

4. *What is the name of the mode from the 5th interval of the Major scale?*

5. *What are the intervals of the Lydian mode?*

6. *Which mode can be regarded as a new key centre for minor keys?*

7. *What is the sequence of triad based chords that we get from the harmonised major scale?*

8. *What is the sequence of triad based chords we get from the harmonised minor scale?*

9. *What is the sequence of 7th chords we get from the harmonised major scale?*

10. *What is the sequence of 7th chords we get from the harmonised minor scale?*

11. *What number system can be used to translate a chord sequence into any key?*

6 Further Techniques

This chapter contains introductions to different kinds of techniques on the Bass. The styles used in the musical examples aren't necessarily the only ones they can be used with.

Slap and Pop

This is a percussive technique for the Bass. It's a bit like a drum kit with the slap as the bass drum and the pop as the snare drum. Although there are a number of different ways it can be done, none of them are the "correct way" it depends what suits you. Here's what I find works best.

Thumb Slap

Hitting the string with the thumb for a booming bass sound. The hand should be postured with the fingers tucked in a bit and the thumb sticking out. The part of the thumb that hits the string should be the side of the joint as shown on the photo to the right…

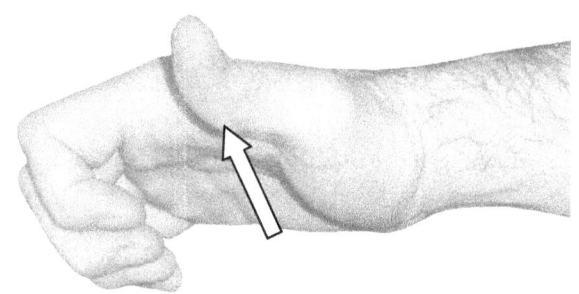

The thumb should be more or less in line with the string on contact (not necessarily on approach). It needs to bounce off the string to let it ring, so don't hold the thumb too rigidly otherwise it may mute the string as soon as it has hit it. The propulsion is in the rotation of the arm / wrist rather than the thumb itself, the thumb follows.

1.

2.

Have a go on the low E string first, then try on the A string which will be a little trickier as you need to avoid hitting other strings above as well as below.

Note: Some explanations will say the thumb should rest on the next string after a slap but initially it is best to concentrate on having a loose thumb not muting the string after contact.

Here's an exercise...

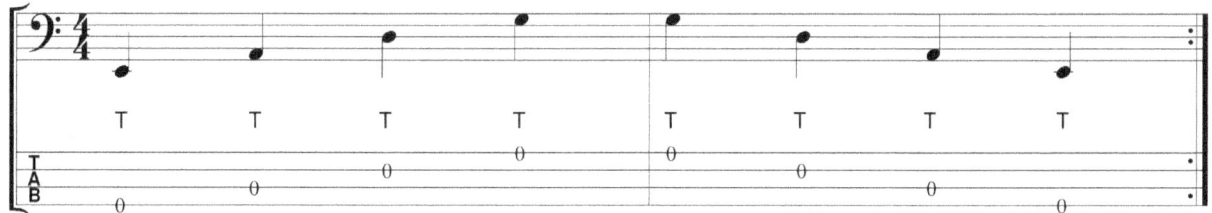

T = Thumb slap

You'll notice it is harder to get as much of a powerful sound from the higher strings (D and G). Thinner strings aren't as responsive to this heavier technique (hence it is used rarely on the 6 string guitar).

Pop

Pull the string out with a finger then release it so the string hits the fret-board for a "popping" sound. You can use your index or middle finger for this.

1.

2.

When using both slaps and pops, use the middle when the pop is at least 2 strings from the slap and the index when the pop is on the next string or the same string as the slap.

Here's an exercise with finger pops...

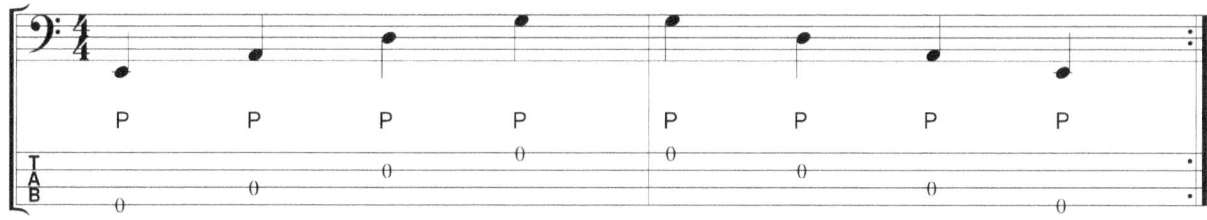

P = Finger Pop

95

Here's a funk riff using thumb slaps. You can use a pop on bar 6 for the open D note if you prefer…

Heist

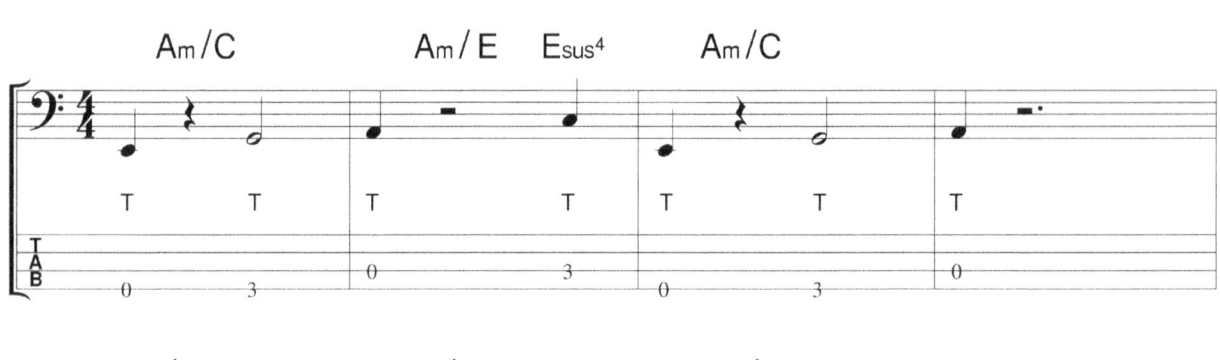

Popping falls into place nicely after a slap because once the hand has come down after the thumb slap, a finger can pop a string on the way back up again. Here's a Motown style riff with slap and pop…

Mo' Slap n Pop

For this funk riff you can alternate between thumb slaps and finger pops as it's written, or use more thumb slaps if you prefer…

70's Mystery

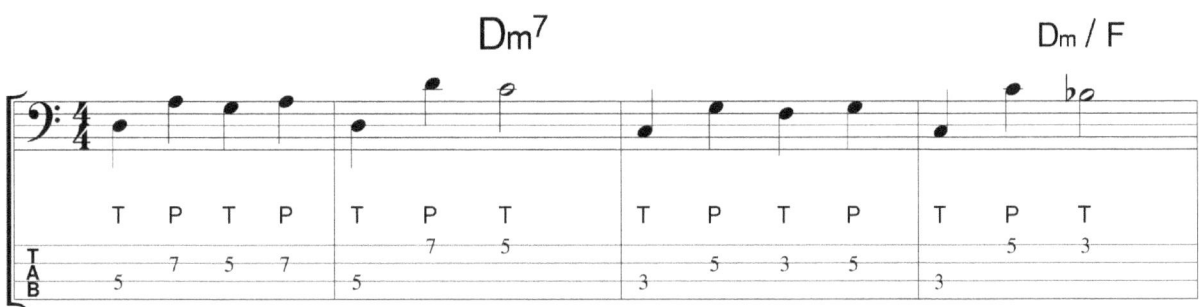

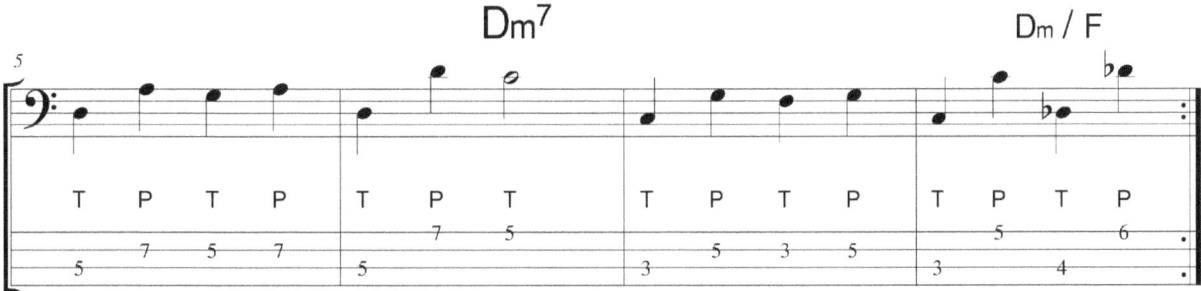

Legato

Notes played smoothly flowing into each other with no silence between. Techniques to achieve this include the hammer-on, pull-off and slide.

Hammer-ons

A hammer-on is placing a fretting finger down on a fret to play a note without plucking the string, as though you are "hammering" on with the finger.

Play the 5th fret of the D string with the index finger.

While this note is ringing use the 3rd finger to hammer onto the 7th fret of the same string.

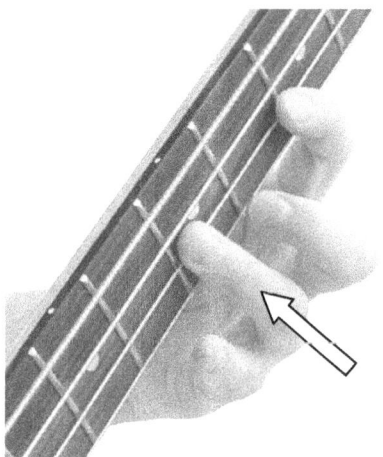

You can use any fingers, string and frets you like (as long as you can reach). Try to place the finger that is hammering on as accurately as you can. Practise at a slow speed at first.

Pull-offs

A pull-off is the opposite of a hammer-on. Pull the finger off the fret where it has just played and as you do, move it down slightly so it plucks the string as it leaves, this will play the note behind (be that an open string or a fretted note). Try not to hit other strings with the finger as it leaves.

A hammer-on is indicated with a curved line from one note to another *higher* note. A pull-off is indicated with a curved line from one note to another *lower* note. Don't confuse them with a tie (covered on page 60), which is a curved line between two notes *of the same pitch*.

The piece on the next page contains hammer-ons and pull-offs…

Flow

Slides

Moving a finger across the frets of a string up or down for a sliding sound, also known as *glissando*. For this your hand can't stay in a fixed position, it needs to move across the neck, so the trick is to stop the slide at the intended fret making sure the hand is stable as it shifts position.

A slide between notes is indicated with a straight line between them. A slide to or from a note is indicated with a straight line to or from it. The following riff has a slide down from the 10th fret low E and a slide from the 4th to 5th fret on the D string.

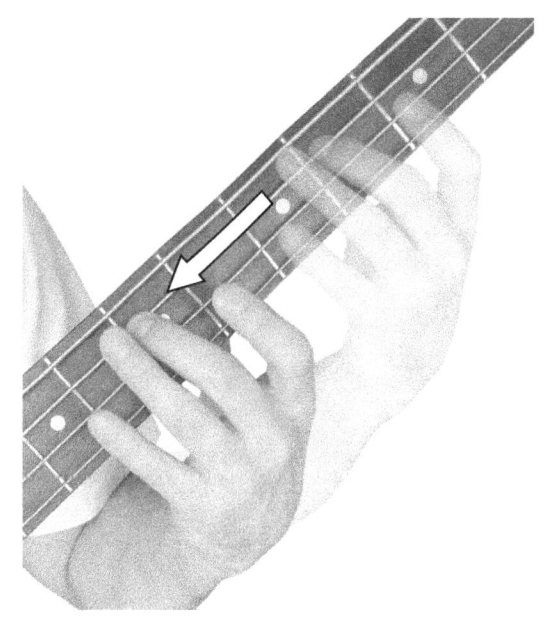

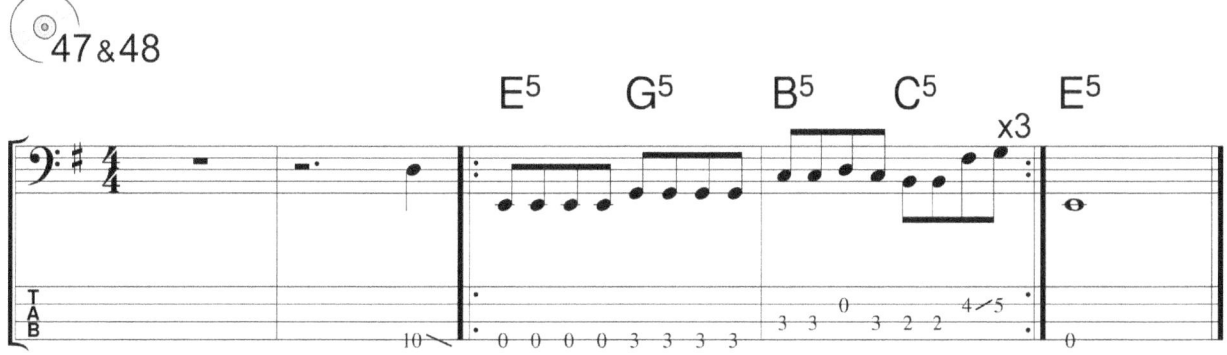

This piece achieves legato with hammer-ons and slides…

This piece uses all three legato techniques with slap and pop…

Slapato

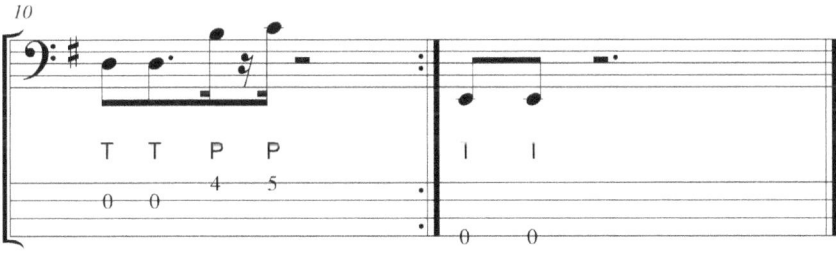

Harmonics

The finger gently touches the string directly above the fret for a sustained chiming sound (Chime; The sound produced by or as if by a bell or bells).

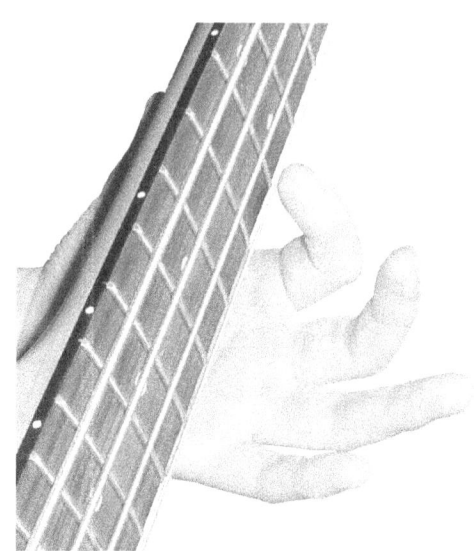

Try this on the 12th fret first. Some points at which harmonics can be found (called *harmonic nodes*) are on the 12th, 9th, 7th, 5th, 4th, 16th, 19th and 24th frets. If you don't have as many as 24 frets the harmonic can still be found at a point on the string where the 24th fret would be.

Harmonics are indicated with a diamond shape. The following exercise has D.C. (as we originally saw for "Calm beach" page 64). *al Fine* means you apply the finish, so end the piece on the repeat where you see the word "Fine" on the end of the 2nd bar.

Encounters of the Harmonic Kind

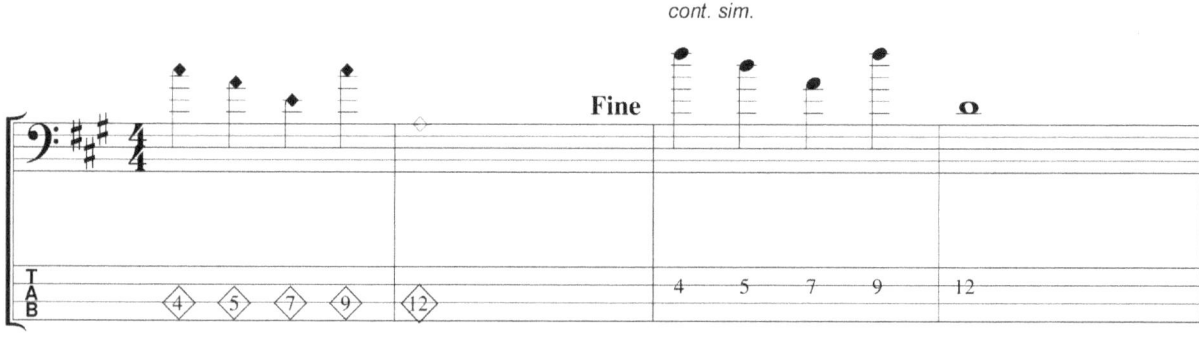

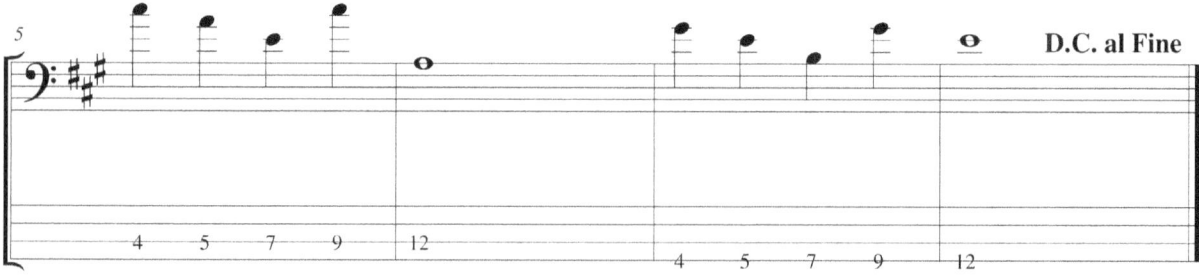

cont. sim. = continue similar (the whole piece uses harmonics)

(There is delay used on the track making it echo but it still works without).

Here's a piece using harmonics with a couple of slides toward the end…

A Day to Remember

This piece uses all three kinds of slides with some harmonics at the end…

Over the Hills and Far Away

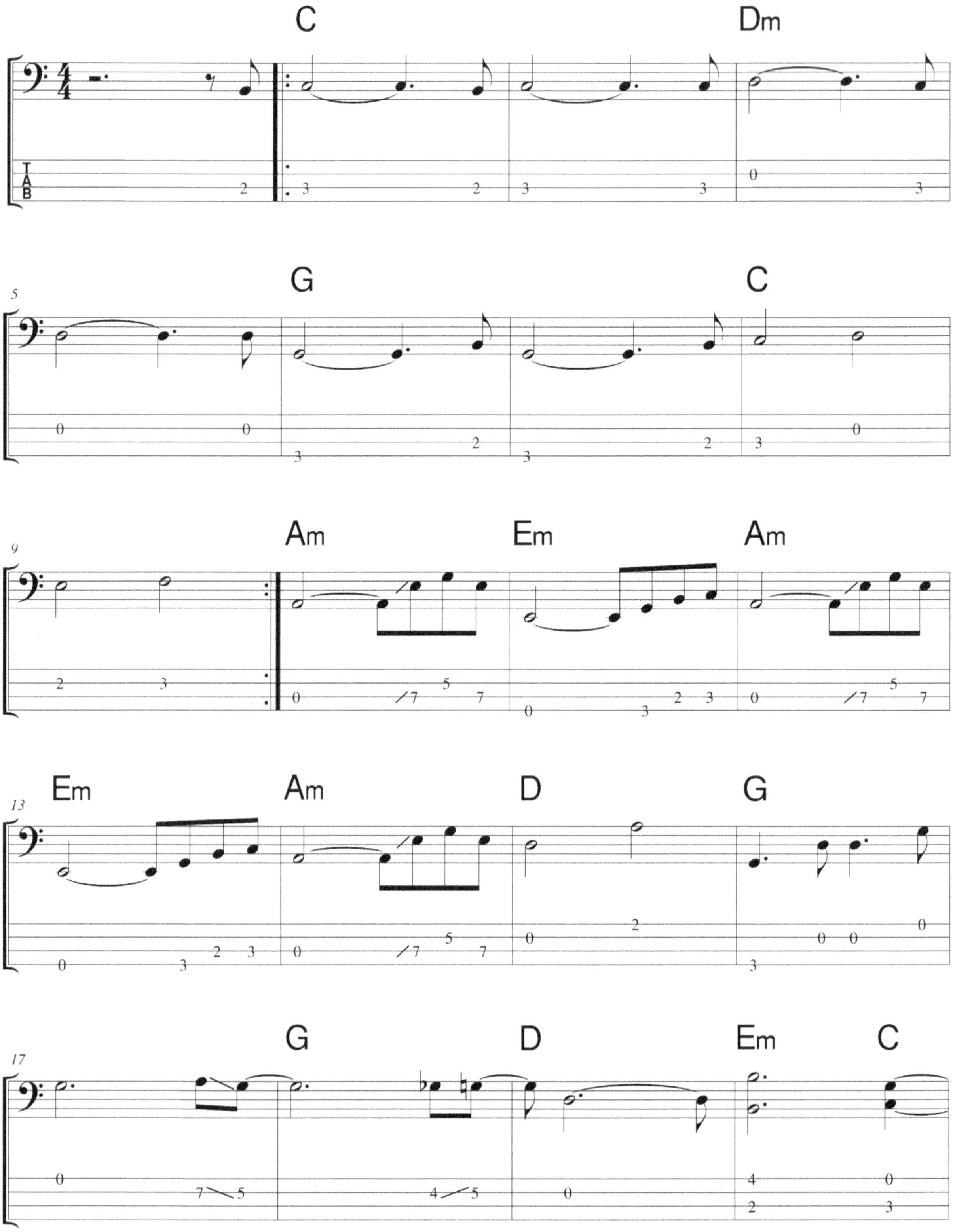

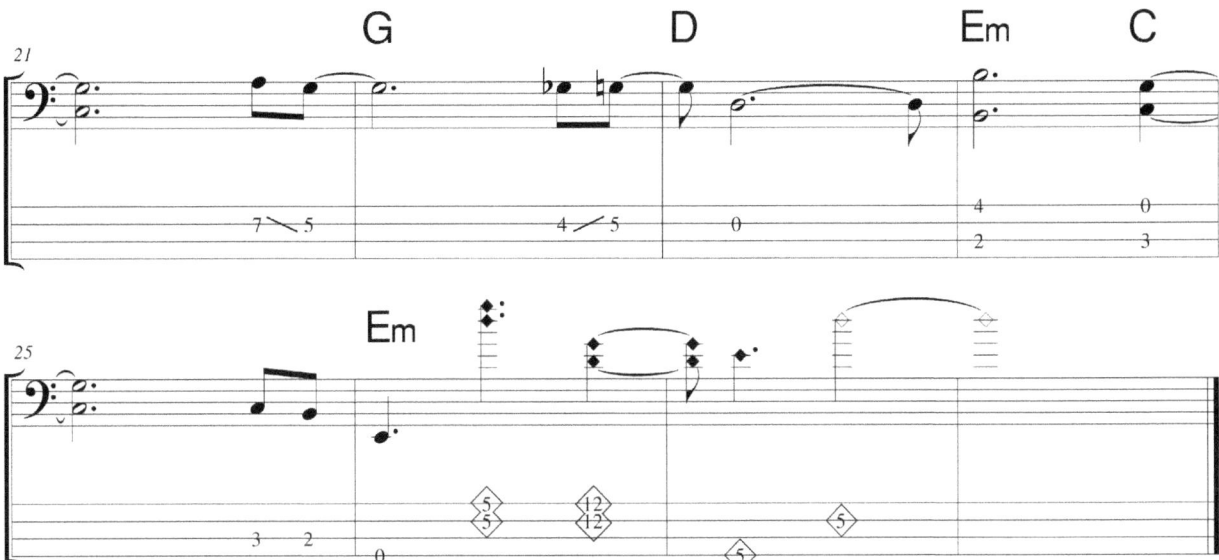

Tapping

Using the plucking hand, place a finger down on a fret (like a hammer-on). Tapping on the Bass can be tricky at first because with thicker strings your finger needs to balance on the string more and not slip off, as opposed to the flesh at the end of your finger surrounding the string as it would for the thinner strings of a 6-string guitar.

In the photo the thumb is propped up above the neck for more control. When moving up and down the fret-board with tapping, the thumb can slide up and down like this to maintain stability for the fingers on the fret-board.

Often when tapping on the Bass both hands are used in conjunction, the fretting hand taps on the lower end of the fret-board for the Bass notes and the plucking hand taps the higher notes further up the fret-board. The pieces in this section are written like this.

Tapped notes are indicated with a circle around them. Can you recognise the A major scale in the following exercise?...

Tapestry

(The sound effect used on the track is a phaser but the piece can still be played without).

This piece requires use of both the index and middle finger for notes tapped by the plucking hand. There is a harmonic at the end for the last note...

Storm before the Calm

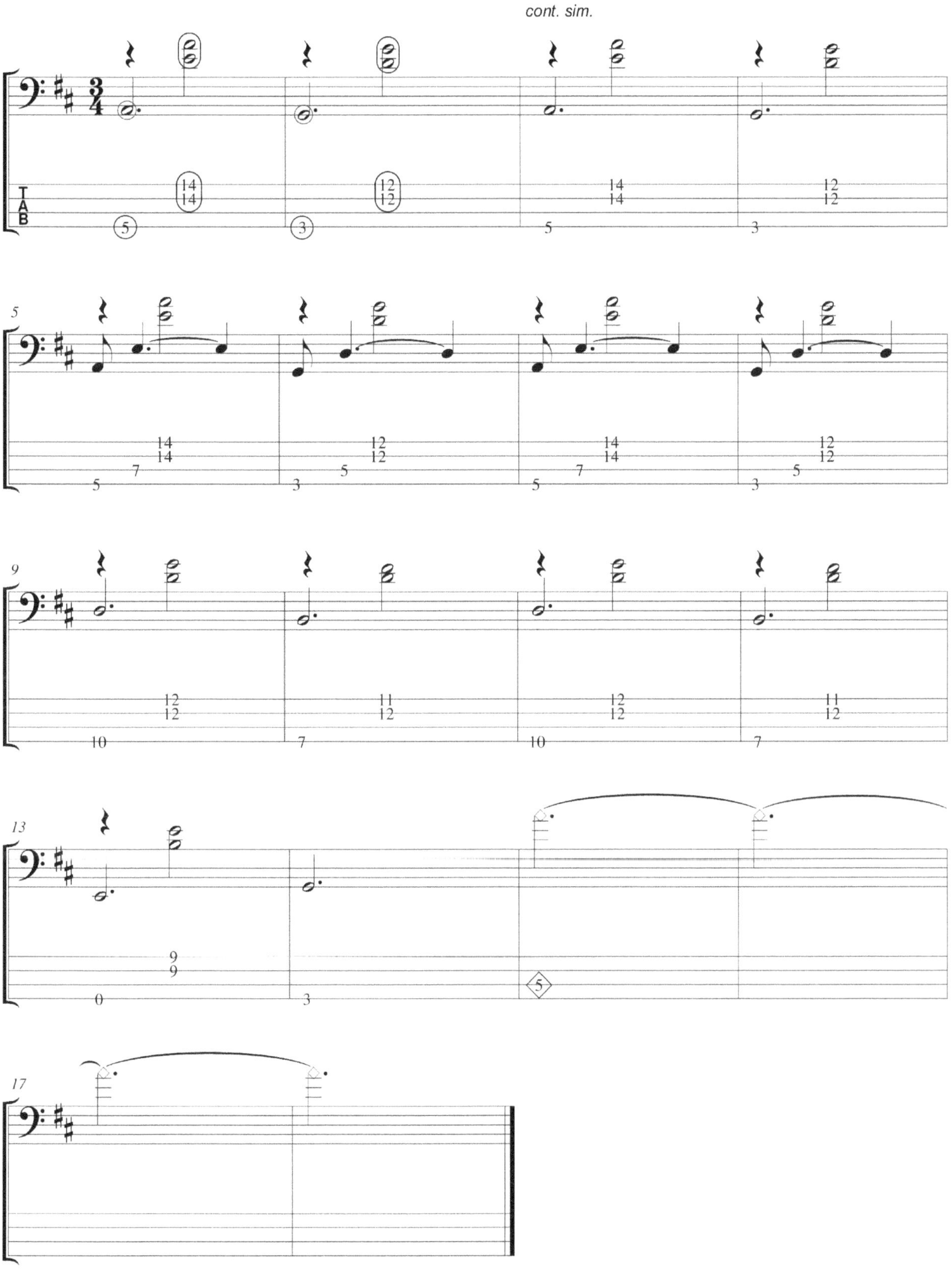

Chapter 6 questions

1. *When thumb slapping, if the thumb mutes the string as soon as it has hit it what are you doing wrong?*

2. *What does **Legato** mean?*

3. *What three methods can be used to achieve Legato?*

4. *What kind of line represents a slide, a curved or straight one?*

5. *Where in relation to the fret should the fretting finger be for a harmonic?*

6. *When tapping, how can the thumb help to add control?*

7. *How are harmonics represented?*

8. *How is tapping represented?*

How to Practise

How much practise? - 30 minutes practise 5 or 6 days a week is better than 2 to 3 hours in one day of the week. If you start to feel that it's a strain physically or mentally and your playing becomes dull, then perhaps it is best to stop and come back later. Full concentration can only last so long, so don't be fooled into ending up confused at how you got something right the first time yet after a while your playing seems to be getting worse. Perhaps it's just that your hand is tired or your concentration is becoming exhausted. Only when something becomes second nature can you continue for longer. Try not to play for more than 10 minutes constantly without a small 1 - 2 minute break and always pay attention to your fingers. If it hurts then stop! if your fingers feel like they are *about* to start "complaining" then have a break for a couple of minutes.

Patience can be fast - Being patient and having time for what might be called "serious boring stuff" is faster than being impatient, doing just the "fun" stuff and your playing not progressing. Rather than just playing around on the Bass with your favourite tunes for 30 minutes, try to spend the first 10 minutes doing technical exercises and / or scales to a metronome. This way you'll progress faster than if you just played for 30 minutes, then the fun stuff becomes more fun because you are better at it rather than reaching a frustrating point where you feel you can't go any further.

Playing Music - A mistake that can be made is trying to play a piece how you want it to sound as opposed to playing it how you are actually able to play it. If you can't play a whole piece well and consistently, you could isolate the more difficult parts and practise them to a metronome at a slower speed at which you can play accurately. As you get better bring it back up to speed until it fits in the song and you can play the whole thing consistently. You can make more improvement in less time this way. The same applies to playing over a backing track, practise without it first.

Likewise for scales, parts of a scale can be harder than other parts. Some might play the hard parts slower and the easier parts faster. If you practise technical exercises / scales to a metronome you develop a sense of tempo and it trains you to play consistently. So play the entire scale at the speed you can play the most difficult part adequately. Playing at a speed too fast for your ability can actually be practising making mistakes and make you worse!

Sense of timing is a skill in its own right - Sometimes less experienced players may tend to play too fast over a slower tempo i.e. a slower piece or a metronome set to a slow speed. Although this may seem contrary to earlier advice, it is often because they are playing to their technical ability rather than concentrating on actually playing in time. Technical ability on it's own means little without a sense of timing. Having your own internal metronome can help keep rhythm, such as tapping your foot to a piece of music.

General

1. Always try to give yourself a slight challenge, not too easy but not too hard either. This way you can make constant progress without getting frustrated or bored repeating the same things you already know.

2. Your own playing should satisfy you to a point that it becomes a positive reinforcement to practising.

3. With something new, try to practise it until you are proficient before moving on. However if something is too hard it's best not to get frustrated. Move on to something else and when you come back to it later you'll be better.

Practise doesn't make perfect, perfect practices makes perfect. It's *quality* not so much quantity that counts!

Stretching Exercises

Stretching can enhance performance and protect against injury such as RSI (repetitive strain injury) that can be common for musicians. If you stretch then it stops your muscles and tendons getting stiff later on. With some of the material covered in this book it would be a good idea to stretch a little before and after. Here are some stretches, don't try to do any of them further than you feel is comfortable...

A. Keep both arms straight and stretch them out while using one hand to hold back the fingers of the other. This stretches the wrist flexors.

B. The hand reversed the other way stretches the wrist extensors.

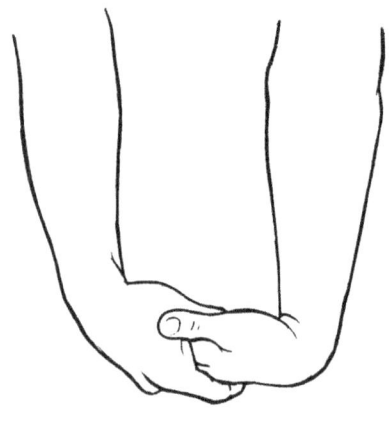
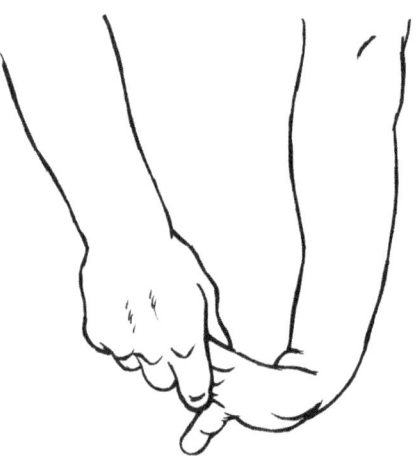

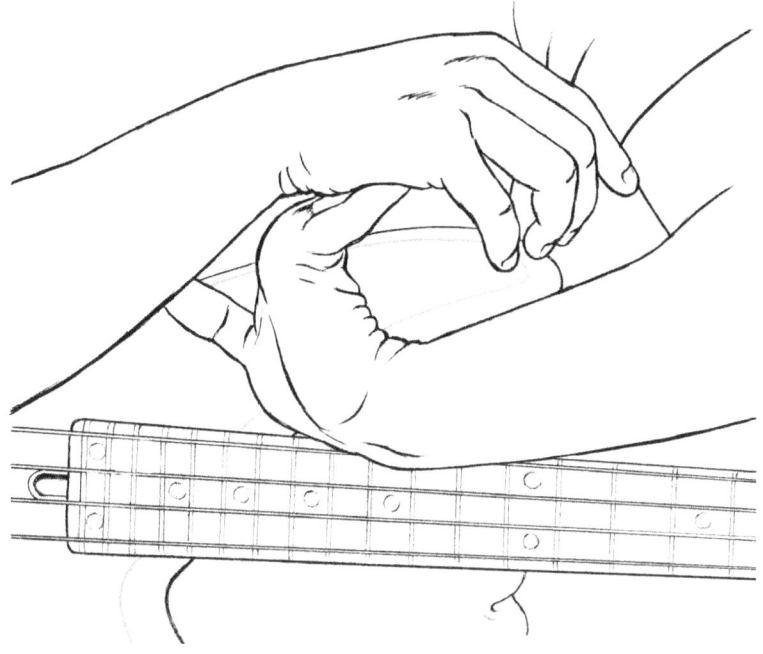

C. If you have the Bass on your lap and want to do a quick stretch, you can easily stretch your hands in front of you.

If you have been sitting with a Bass guitar for a while it can affect your upper back. This is the stiffest area of the back and often becomes even less mobile with a sustained position.

D. Lean backward over the back of a strong enough chair and hold this position for 10 seconds, repeat this 5 times. Putting a rolled up magazine or towel behind your upper back can help. This stretch flexes your back the opposite way that it would have been while playing Bass.

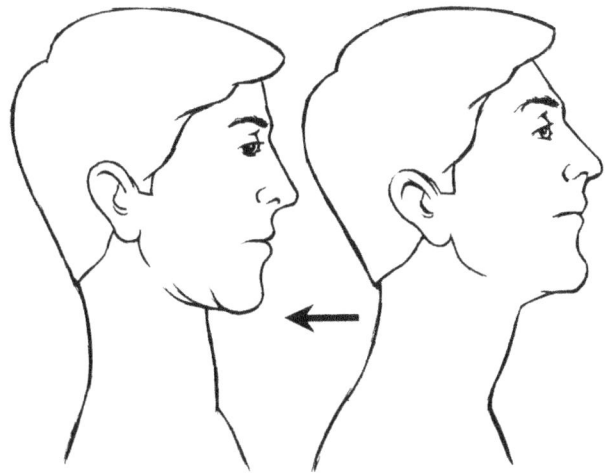

E. This counteracts the forward head posture that can develop in musicians. Tuck your chin in gently and pull your head back gently. This is best done while sitting upright.

F. The following stretch keeps the Median nerve mobile. The Median nerve controls some of the main finger flexors. This stretch is good for playing where strength is generally needed such as the Bass guitar, which requires more pressure to push down on the frets.

1. Start with your shoulder down and elbow bent with your thumb pointing backwards.

2. Slowly extend your whole arm keeping your shoulder down and wrist bent backward until you can feel reasonable tension in your forearm. Repeat this up to six times.

Qigong balls – two iron balls of about 1.5" in diameter that you circulate around each other in your palm. You could try it clockwise and counter clockwise, one way will be harder than the other. This flow-like motion of the finger joints with minimum force makes the hand muscles feel smoother and is good for repetitive strain injury. This can also be good for your hand if you use a computer mouse, as are stretches D and E if you sit at a computer.

How to String a Bass

Strings come in different thickness (known as *gauges*). On a set of medium strings the G string would be "45" which is 0.045 inches in diameter (450 thousands of an inch), strings D to low E would be 65, 85, 105. A light set from G to low E would be 40, 60, 80, 100, while a heavy set would be 50, 75, 95, 110. The gauge sequence can vary slightly depending on the manufacturer.

Bass guitar strings have a metal hoop on one end. It is the opposite sharp end that goes through the corresponding hole on the bridge. Make sure you get the right string for the right hole.

That's the simple bit out of the way. Next the head of the Bass where the tuning pegs are. Stringing a Bass guitar is a bit different to how you would string a 6-string guitar because you need to clip the strings to size (with pliers) before they go onto the tuning pegs.

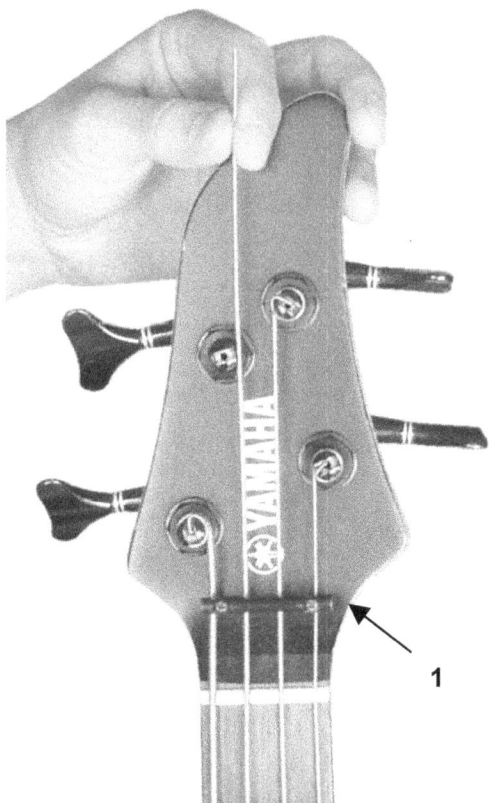

Each tuning peg has a hole through its middle for the end of the Bass string to go into. The strings should be cut to length so that when finally wound tight it's not wound around the peg too few or too many times.

On the picture to the left the A string has been cut so that when held straight it passes its peg by 3½ inches. For some sets of strings the ends are equal in diameter and generally thinner, however if this is not the case with your set then bear in mind that the thicker the string is the less times you can wind it around the peg, while thinner strings can be wound around the peg a few times more as long as it's not so many it starts to look untidy. I would recommend 3 inches past the peg for thicker strings and 4 inches past the peg for thinner strings, and don't forget to pass the string under the string rail (1).

In the first photo the string is placed into the hole of the peg. Put it in as far as it will go. The string can be wound around the peg to save time winding (as shown in the second photo) although Bass strings are reasonably thick anyway so you won't have far to go.

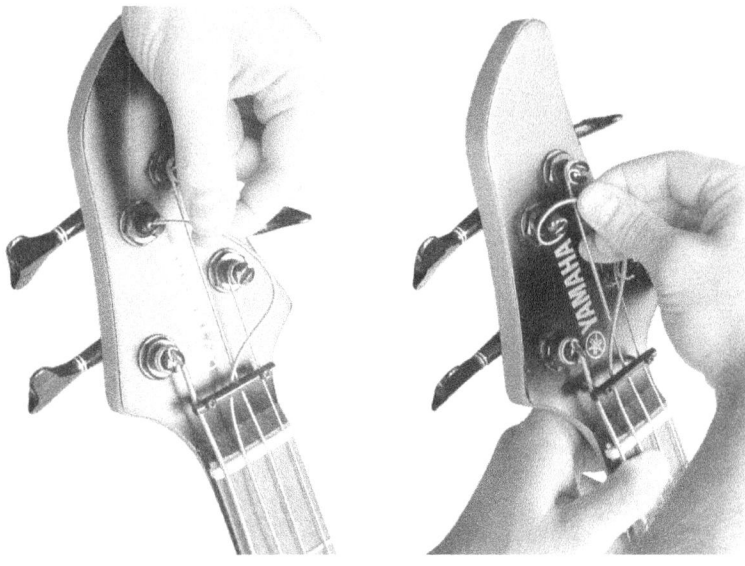

Before we go any further and tighten the pegs there are some important things to consider.

The diagram below shows what we are aiming for. The string has been wrapped downward of the peg. This increases the angle of the string over the nut making it more secure within it (2)...

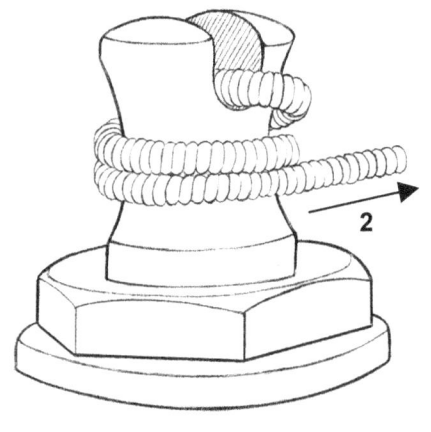

In the diagrams below we can see that the strings should come out on the side of the peg that makes them as straight as possible when looking at the Bass face-on. This is especially important for pegs that are closer to the nut because if the string comes out on the wrong side, it will push sideways within the nut (3).

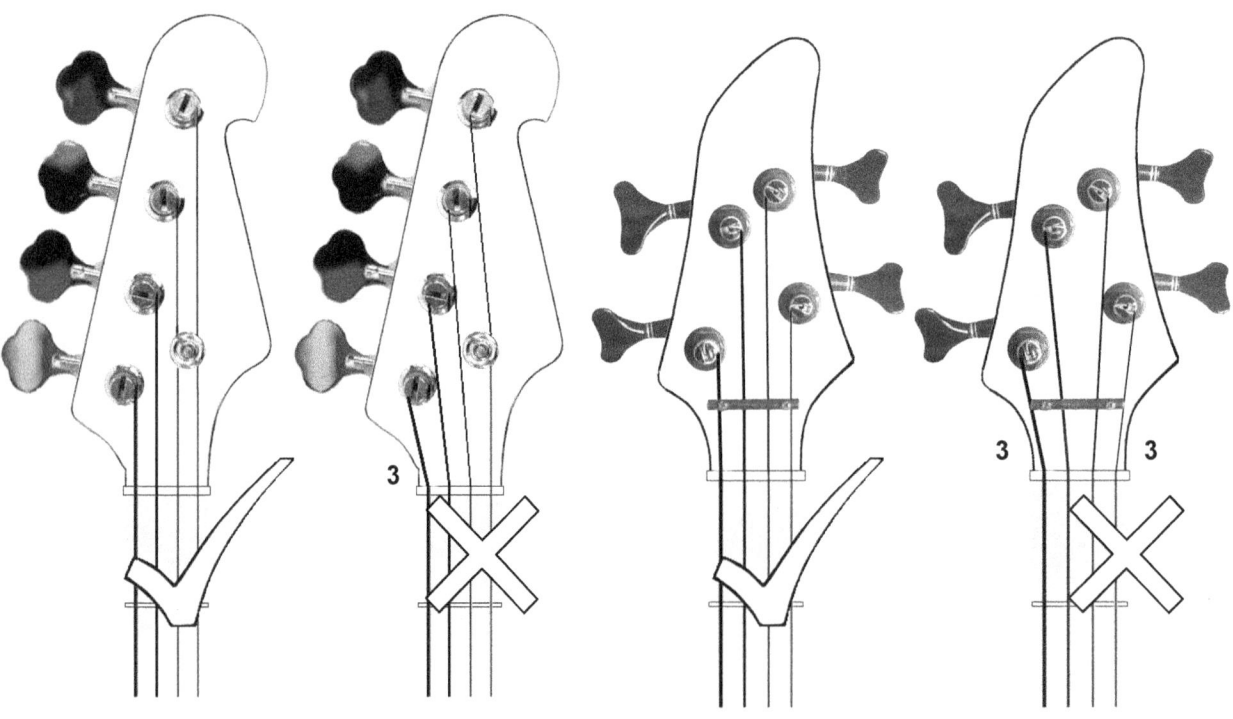

114

With all this in mind we can start to tighten the peg. Hold the guitar as follows…

The feet steady the Bass while the neck rests on the leg leaving the hands free.

Below is a close up of what the hands should be doing. The thumb is used to push the string down onto the head of the guitar (**4**) while the fingers pull the string up gently (**5**) to give it tension so it stays in place around the peg while it is tightened…

Once all the strings are on you can tune your Bass and you're ready to play.

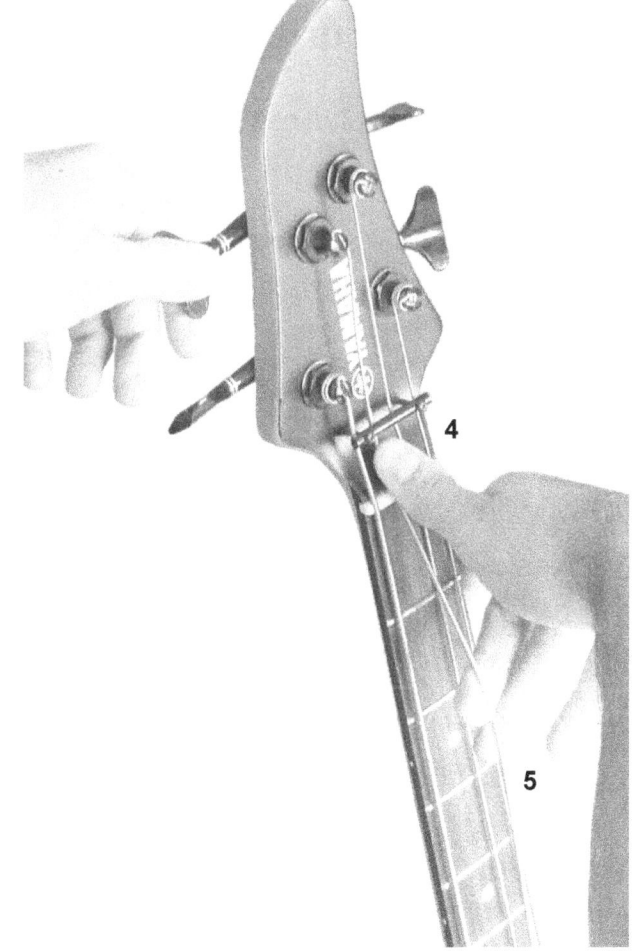

115

Answers

Chapter 1 - The Beginning (page 21)

1. Just behind the fret
2. To match conventional notation, also it's what you see when looking down at your Bass
3. Rhythm
4. Resting on top of the pick-up
5. The middle finger because it's a bit longer and reaches the string first
6. When moving from a higher string to a lower one
7. The wrist / muscle at the base of the thumb area of the hand rests on the guitar.
8. Roughly central to the opposing fingers

Chapter 2 - Fundamentals (page 49)

1. Enharmonic equivalent
2. Two frets
3. One fret
4. The same note at a higher or lower pitch
5. Tone, Tone, Semitone, Tone, Tone, Tone, Semitone
6. D
7. G♯
8. B
9. Arches for downward picking, points for upward picking
10. Low, Mid and Upper
11. No
12. Yes
13. Root, 3rd and 5th
14. Root, ♭3rd and 5th

Chapter 3 - Reading Rhythm (page 66)

1. How long a note lasts
2. Four
3. Two
4. How many beats per bar
5. What kind of note value for the beat
6. Six eighth note beats per bar
7. An eighth note
8. Two
9. Quarter note rest
10. They are joined together
11. The strongest beats

12. By half
13. A Tie
14. It's a dotted whole note so it would last for six quarter notes (or three half notes)
15. Only one note, the second note extends the length of time of the first.

Chapter 4 - 7th Arpeggios (page 75)

1. Root, 3rd, 5th and 7th
2. Root ♭3rd, 5th and ♭7th
3. Root, 3rd, 5th and ♭7th
4. Mid
5. Upper
6. Da Capo "From the head" or "Go back to the beginning"
7. It's a coda, once you see *al coda* (which means apply the coda) it acts like a teleport taking you from where you see the first one to the next.

Chapter 5 - Modes and Harmony

Roman Numerals (pages 89 - 92)…

Major keys

1) Em, A, D, G
2) Cm, F, B♭, E♭
3) E♭m, A♭, D♭, G♭
4) Cmaj^7, Fmaj^7, Bm$^{7♭5}$, Am^7
5) Amaj^7, Dmaj^7, G♯m$^{7♭5}$, F♯m^7
6) Fmaj^7, B♭maj^7, Em$^{7♭5}$, Dm^7
7) Gm^7, Cm, Fm, B♭^{7}
8) D♯m^7, G♯m, C♯m, F♯^{7}
9) Bm^7, Em, Am, D^7

Minor keys

10) F♯m, Emaj^7, B^7, C♯m^7
11) Gm, Fmaj^7, C^7, Dm^7
12) Em, Dmaj^7, A^7, Bm^7
13) F♯m$^{7♭5}$, C, B^7, Em
14) C♯m$^{7♭5}$, G, F♯^{7}, Bm
15) Dm$^{7♭5}$, A♭, G^7, Cm

Chapter 5 questions (page 93)

1. Mode
2. The Parent scale
3. Dorian

4. Mixolydian
5. Root, 2nd 3rd, $\sharp4^{th}$, 5th, 6th, 7th
6. Aeolian (Natural minor)
7. Major, minor, minor, Major, Major, minor, diminished
8. minor, diminished, Major, minor, minor, Major, Major
9. Maj7^{th}, min7^{th}, min7^{th}, Maj7^{th}, Dom7^{th}, min7^{th}, min$7^{\flat}5$
10. min7^{th}, min$7^{\flat}5$, Maj7^{th}, min7^{th}, min7^{th}, Maj7^{th}, Dom7^{th}
11. Roman numerals

Chapter 6 - Further Techniques (page 108)

1. Holding the thumb too rigid
2. Notes played smoothly flowing into each other
3. Hammer-on, Pull-off, Slide
4. A straight line
5. Directly above it
6. The thumb can be propped up on the neck
7. With a diamond shape
8. With a circle

All songs (except for Bayou Noir) composed by Gareth Evans

Guitar played by Gareth Evans on tracks 1, 2, 19, 20, 21, 22, 23, 24, 25, 26, 27, 28, 39, 40, 41, 42, 43, 44, 45, 46, 47, 48, 49, 50, 51, 52, 54, 55, 56, 57.

Bass played by Gareth Evans on tracks 1, 3, 5, 7, 9, 11, 13, 15, 17, 19, 21, 23, 25, 27, 29, 31, 33, 35, 37, 39, 40, 41, 43, 45, 47, 49, 51, 53, 54, 56, 58, 59.

Drums programmed by Gareth Evans on tracks 1, 2, 19, 20, 21, 22, 23, 24, 25, 26, 27, 28, 39, 40, 41, 42, 43, 44, 45, 46, 47, 48, 49, 50, 51, 52, 54, 55, 56, 57, 59, 60.

Real Band (PG music) used for backing band on tracks 3, 4, 5, 6, 7, 8, 9, 10, 11, 12, 13, 14, 15, 16, 17, 18, 29, 30, 31, 32, 33, 34, 35, 36, 37, 38.

Copyright © 2013 by Intuition Publications

www.ingramcontent.com/pod-product-compliance
Lightning Source LLC
Chambersburg PA
CBHW081418300426
44109CB00019BA/2344